HINDUISM
A Way of Life

HINDUISM
A Way of Life

SITANSU S. CHAKRAVARTI

MOTILAL BANARSIDASS PUBLISHERS
PRIVATE LIMITED • DELHI

First Published: 1991
Reprint: Delhi, 1992, 1994

© Sitansu S. Chakravarti
All rights reserved. No part of this publication may be
reproduced in any form, or by any means, without
written permission of the publishers.

MOTILAL BANARSIDASS PUBLISHERS PRIVATE LIMITED

ISBN: 81-208-0927-0 (Cloth)
ISBN: 81-208-0899-1 (Paper)

Also available at:
MOTILAL BANARSIDASS
41 U.A. Bungalow Road, Jawahar Nagar, Delhi 110 007
120 Royapettah High Road, Mylapore, Madras 600 004
16 St. Mark's Road, Bangalore 560 001
Ashok Rajpath, Patna 800 004
Chowk, Varanasi 221 001

PRINTED IN INDIA
BY JAINENDRA PRAKASH JAIN AT SHRI JAINENDRA PRESS,
A-45 NARAINA, PHASE I, NEW DELHI 110 028
AND PUBLISHED BY NARENDRA PRAKASH JAIN FOR
MOTILAL BANARSIDASS PUBLISHERS PVT. LTD.,
BUNGALOW ROAD, DELHI 110 007

To the memory of my father
CHINTAHARAN DEVASHARMA
who was my teacher till the end of his life
and a true friend

Contents

Foreword by Joseph T. O'Connell		9
Acknowledgements		13
Introduction		15

I THE HINDU WAY OF LIFE

1	Some Basic Features of Hinduism	23
2	Hindu Sacraments and Rituals	29
3	Some Relevant Information	33
4	Festivals	36
5	Hindu Worship: The Sequential Pattern	40
6	Meaning of Icons	44
7	Mantras and Prayers for Various Occasions	55

II HINDU SPIRITUALITY

8	The Philosophy of Hindu Spirituality	63
9	Chaplaincy in the Hindu Tradition	67
10	The Human Value System—Ethics and Religion: The Hindu Perspective	69

III HINDUS IN NORTH AMERICA

11	Hindus in North America	79
	Appendix A: Hinduism and Other World Religions	84
	Appendix B: Centres of Hindu Spirituality in North America	86
	Notes	89
	Glossary	91
	Bibliography	101
	Index	103

Foreword

Hindu religious life has received its fair share of weighty scholarly treatment over the last two centuries. And there has been a massive effusion of testimonial and apologetic writing in English on diverse ways of being Hindu. What have not been readily available, however, are succinct, sensibly focused introductions to Hindu religion (and Hindu culture and society) immediately relevant to persons encountering Hindus in the course of their work in the professions of human service: e.g., doctors and nurses, teachers and school administrators, social workers, police, lawyers, correctional officers, judges and chaplains.

This situation is especially unfortunate for first generation immigrants. It is precisely to members of such professions that many immigrants, especially the needy and others in difficulty, must look for help and understanding. Yet in both Canada and the United States very few members of these professions have had any significant personal contact with Hindus, or more than the most cursory acquaintance with the Hindu tradition through study or reading.

Dr Sitansu S. Chakravarti, himself an immigrant resident of many years in the greater Toronto area, has set himself the task of narrowing the gap between what is actually known (to scholars and articulate Hindus) about Hindu life and what is accessible in reasonable convenient format to persons hard pressed for time, yet needing practical advice on how to relate well to clients, patients or other individuals who are Hindu. He has begun the task quite well, which is not surprising in view of his rich and interesting background. There is, of course, his own professional training in Eastern and Western philosophy (Ph. D., Syracuse) and his teaching at the University of Rajasthan. There is also a family tradition of interpreting the Hindu tradition, as exemplified by his father, the late Chintaharan Chakravarti, renowned scholar of Hindu Tantra. Moreover, the family of his wife, Rina (herself a teacher and author of a recent textbook on Bengali language), reinforces the Chakravartis' verve for maintaining and advancing the Indian cultural heritage. Rina's mother, Sampriti Devi, whose illustrations embellish this volume, is both artist and writer and sister of the noted Bengali film-maker, Ritwik Ghatak. Added to this stimulating family environment is the varied practical experience that Dr Chakravarti has acquired through work as chaplain, speaker, dialogue participant, and resource person in varied multicultural situations in Canada.

This concise book reflects the complexity and perceptiveness of its author. Dr Chakravarti is a Hindu Brahmin born in India, but he has passed most of his adult years in North America among those who are not Hindu. He is an academic by training but has gained practical human experience in other professions as well. He is involved in the work of Hindu religious organizations, and is acquainted with Hindu spiritual exercises, but has a positive appreciation of the intellectual orientation of the atheist. In particular he is at pains to report to modern readers about classical Hindu forms of non-theist and atheist thought and spiritual discipline. Indeed it is this interesting treatment of spirituality that gives this book a distinctive quality, over and above its practical usefulness.

For all its brevity and selectivity, *Hinduism: A Way of Life* covers a good deal of ground. It contains essential information on standard Hindu sacraments and rituals, on dress codes, customs and festivals, on worship practices and sacred images. It provides a sampler of prayers, points for reflection and liturgical formulae. It notes peculiarities of emigré Hindu experience in the United States and Canada and incorporates insights from the author's experience as a Hindu chaplain (surely a rare if not unique perspective in this part of the world). The most substantial and interesting, for me at least, portions of the book are those where Dr Chakravarti offers in brief compass his studied reflections on Hindu philosophy, ethics and spirituality. The glossary is also a significant section of the book and should be browsed.

The task before Dr Chakravarti and a generation of practical interpreters of the Hindu way of life as salient in specific professional contexts is a daunting one and will not quickly or easily be brought to completion. It is high time persons of Sitansu Chakravarti's qualifications, experience and personal command of the issues begin the work. The present book is a commendable pioneering effort in this task and should be of assistance, as well as interest, to many.

Department of Religious Studies JOSEPH T. O'CONNELL
University of Toronto

Acknowledgements

Thanks are due to Mrs Asha Bhai and Mr Laikh Ram Singh for typing arrangements for earlier drafts of the manuscript. But for Shivabrata (Shanku), my 'other son', a computer adept in his teens, the final version could not have been prepared. I am thankful to Professor T. Venkatacharya, Department of Linguistics, University of Toronto, for help regarding references of some Sanskrit passages and their transliteration. I would like to mention my indebtedness to Buddhadev Bhattacharya for his kind and meticulous help at every step of the publication of the book. Special thanks are due to Madhav Upadhyay of Hindu Prarthana Samaj, Toronto and Robert Heard of Toronto Public Library for providing constant help and encouragement. Mr Heard has greatly assisted in the final editing of the work. The author is also very thankful to Leslie McGrath, Librarian, Toronto Public Library, for making useful suggestions for improvement, and for taking a special interest in the publication of the manuscript. Thanks are due to Bruce Adlum of the Peel Board of Education for introducing the book in his World Religions Class, and giving useful feedback. Professor Joseph T. O'Connell, Department of Religious Studies, University of Toronto, has kindly written the Foreword to the book and made many useful suggestions. Swami Tathagatananda, Head of the Vedanta Society of New York, Swami Prabuddhananda, Head of the Vedanta Society of Northern California, and Swami Adishwarananda, Head of the Ramakrishna Vivekananda Centre of New York, have kindly gone through the book and made a number of valuable suggestions. Words cannot express the author's appreciation to Swami Brahmananda, former Rector, Bharat Sevashram Sangha Hindu Temple, Toronto, who showered his constant affection and blessings on him and eagerly awaited the completion of the book. The author deeply regrets his passing away, all the more as he will not have the chance of presenting the finished book to this monk, who was a personification of love and tenderness.

Introduction

Although there has been an opening up to Eastern mysticism, including Hinduism, in North America in recent times, the knowledge of the religion is sporadic, and amounts to such coinage as *karma, trinity, guru* or *Vedanta*. Again, books that people base their 'knowledge' of Hinduism on do not always provide the right information or convey the right spirit of the religion as it is lived and practised by more than 600 million people all the world over.

The doctrine of *karma*, which goes hand in hand with the theory that we had previous births, should not be taken as the main teaching of Hinduism. The goal of the religion is, by far, the realization of one's true nature, and not the occult search for one's identity in the past life. Atheism is accepted as an alternate way of spirituality in the religion, as we will see in the book. The genuine *guru (sad-guru)* is looked upon as the representative of God for theists, making the aspirant ready for the knowledge of his relation to the Supreme. To the atheist, he is the most important person, helping the aspirant to his self-realization. Either way, the *guru* is supposed to have a very special place in one's life.

Each book on Hinduism contributes its share to the 'trinity' of the religion that supposedly brings it, in some indeterminate way, close to Christianity. In fact, in a world religions class that I was called upon to address some time ago, I heard it said that this is a common area between both religions. The trinity of Hinduism, which comprises Brahma, Vishnu and Shiva, i.e., gods in charge of creation, preservation and destruction respectively, catering to the concept of division of labour in the realm of spirituality, has been, unknown to many scholars in the Western world, virtually obsolete for quite some time. There are two reasons for this: (1) Brahma, the first member of the trinity, is very much less prominent in the Hindu pantheon than in earlier times. There is only one temple in India, in Pushkar, Rajasthan, dedicated to the god. In the process of the evolution of the religion, he has virtually disappeared except as a matter of historical legacy. (2) Vishnu and Shiva, the other two members of the trinity, have become responsible for all the three functions themselves in their individual capacities. Thus, the idea of division of labour on which the concept of the trinity is based is no longer in operation. Instead of three, the Hindus have five now, all of whom are but various manifestations of the One.

Hinduism is not a single faith, but a religion with a single pattern of faiths. *Vedanta*, of the absolute monistic kind (i.e., *Advaita Vedanta*), belongs to this pattern. Thus, it does not exhaust Hinduism, reducing the other faiths in the religion to a questionable status, nor should it be considered as separate from the religion. It represents a faith based on one of the diverse interpretations of the Hindu scriptures, the *Upanishads*, that form part of the *Vedas*.

Hinduism is accepted as a force in today's Western world through *yoga* and *meditation*, that many Hindu *gurus* and *swamis* in their ochre robes are busy teaching all over the world. A general eagerness to have some understanding of the religion is on the rise. It is also the case that a sizeable number of Hindus have adopted North America as their home during the course of the last two decades. These people are hospitalized when sick, attend old peoples' homes reaching the right age, and their children go to local schools. The chaplains taking care of the inmates of public institutions have to have some knowledge of the religion in order to be able to offer those belonging to the Hindu fold any service. The Boards of Education need to be conversant with the broad religious practices of the pupils, the expectations and aspirations of the parents, and, above all, the life-style of the people which is, both covertly and overtly, grounded in their religion. Teachers are expected to know the background of their pupils, including their religious tradition, especially when values are taught in the class, to ensure, among other things, that a dichotomy does not exist for the children between home and school. Multicultural bodies, too, need some information about the people they are going to serve.

This book is designed to satisfy the needs of people of all these diverse kinds, including those practising the religion, who might be looking for some authentic information on it for themselves as well as for their children. The *mantras* and passages in the original Sanskrit have been included, so that these could be used on the proper occasions. There are English translations following the originals to help those who do not understand Sanskrit. Chaplains will find the book useful. Although it is not a manual for Hindu rites and rituals, they will find some hints on ministering to the dying or sick, when a Hindu priest is unavailable. There are universal prayers included here that can be used for inter-faith services. Chapter 9, *Chaplaincy in The Hindu Tradition*, is meant specifically for the use of chaplains. Teachers and Boards of Education will find the text, especially Chapter 11, *Hindus in North America*, useful. The latter grew out of several presentations to teachers of the Peel and Halton Boards of Education in Ontario. Chapter 10, *The Human Value System: Ethics and Religion—A Hindu Perspective*, would be relevant for value education. It is the outcome of a talk given at the annual conference of chaplains of Ontario in 1987. Some of the universal prayers can be included in the school prayers. The whole book would be useful to multicultural bodies, and people wishing to have some knowledge of Hinduism as it is practised. Students and teachers of world religions at high school or undergraduate levels will find this book helpful, too. Chapter 8, *The Hindu Philosophy of Spirituality*, adds a philosophical dimension to the book, which, the author believes, is an important perspective for understanding of the religion. Philosophy has been a part and parcel of the religion since ancient times. The rational support of philosophy has provided the necessary ingredients for a free flow of the diverse trends in the religion without giving rise to group enmity leading to religious war.

A general approach to a rational explanation of concepts and customs has been followed throughout the book. The symbolism in four of the main icons of the religion—Ganesha, Shakti, Shiva and Krishna—has been explained in some details which, hopefully, would make the concept of Hindu worship much clearer in conjunction with the section *Hindu Worship—A Sequential Pattern*. Explanations have been given of such well-known customs as the prevalence of vegetarianism among most Hindus, and not eating beef among traditional meat-eaters.

It is customary to characterize Hinduism as not so much a religion as a way of life. Of course it is a way of life, but this fact does not make it any less of a religion. To be precise, this very feature makes Hinduism all the richer a religion, so that it has been described as quite unique in being a personalized religion, as we will see in the text itself. The religion has no founder. Many of the scriptures are anonymous. Their dates vary several centuries, if not millennia, in scholars' accounts. The Hindu ideal has always been to downplay the ego, and dedicate all action to the will of God. Thus, although authoring a book has been considered important, mentioning the name of the author has, many a time, not been seen as appropriate. With the offering of the little ego on the altar of the universal self, i.e., God, for centuries, the Hindu lost also his love for historical details. In spite of the drawbacks that the process might have had on him in history, he has not yet forgotten his goal of reaching to a universal unity beyond all differences, where the small ego falls off, as Sri Ramakrishna says, like the bark of the coconut tree, leaving only its mark of a past existence behind.

The concept of surrendering to the will of God has its echo in the Lord's Prayer of the Christian tradition where the aspirant says: 'Thy will be done.' There are several concepts in Hinduism that have parallels in other religions. I will mention here a few more similarities that I find between the religion and Christianity. Such understanding of commonalities between religions, I believe, will go a long way to the realization of a common spiritual pursuit in man in all his diverse ways.

There is no concept in Hinduism corresponding to that of the *original sin*, but there is one of the *original ignorance* (*mulavidya*) which has similarities with the former. The Judaeo-Christian traditions might be misunderstood as discouraging knowledge, for eating the fruit of the tree of knowledge, we are told, led to the fall of Adam and Eve from Heaven. Knowledge, however, has to be understood as being of two kinds: discursive, as is to be found in science, and spiritual, which goes beyond the domain of reason, in being of the nature of realization, rather than of intellectual understanding. The former is called *apara*, and the latter *para* in the Hindu tradition. Discursive knowledge, however useful it be, even in religious matters, does not lead to the ultimate union with God. The computer significantly called 'Apple', showing part of the fruit eaten off, suggests its connection with the former kind of knowledge. Knowledge generated from the reading of the scriptures with the right attitude is of the other kind.

According to Christianity, Jesus is looked upon as the incarnation of God in flesh and blood, a bridge, as it were, between the mundane world we live in since the Fall and Heaven, the abode of God. The concept of divine incarnation is very much there in Hinduism, too, though Hindus do not believe in only one such incarnation. Rama and Krishna are accepted as the principal incarnations of God according to the Hindu tradition. The portrait of Jesus is placed along with theirs in many a Hindu home.

In both traditions the body is looked upon as the temple where the Lord dwells.

The constant dialogues that I used to have with my father, the late Chintaharan Devasharma, who was a devout Hindu and a great scholar on the religion, have been a continuous source of inspiration toward the writing of this book. His Bengali and English writings have been immensely useful. All this very much reminds me of the continuance of family traditions, cherished so dearly among Hindus. In the words of Kalidasa, the famous Sanskrit poet of India, '. . . The young one did not deviate from his cause (the father), even as the lighted candle does not from its source.'

I apologize for not having used the diacritical marks for transliteration. In some places, however, I have found it necessary to use two consecutive *a*'s in the same word in order to convey the phonetic value of long *a* as in *father*.

Cultural Understanding Everywhere SITANSU S. CHAKRAVARTI
3187 Morning Star Drive
Mississauga, Ontario
Deepavali, October 17, 1990

I

THE HINDU WAY OF LIFE

From the high spiritual flights of the Vedanta philosophy, of which the latest discoveries of science seem like echoes, to the . . . ideas of idolatry with its multifarious mythology, the agnosticism of the Buddhists and the atheism of the Jains, each and all have a place in the Hindu's religion.

SWAMI VIVEKANANDA

1

Some Basic Features of Hinduism

GOD: THE ONE IN MANY

Hinduism is a monotheistic religion which believes that God manifests Himself or Herself in several forms.[1] One is supposed to worship the form that is most appealing to the individual without being disrespectful to other forms of worship. The religion has evolved through thousands of years with a spirit of tolerance toward different ways of spiritual fulfilment.[2] This explains why Hinduism does not propagate conversion to or from other religions, for it holds that religions are alternate ways of worshipping the same divine principle, and thus should not be claiming monopoly of spiritual wisdom. Hinduism believes in a continuity, on a graded scale, of religious practices, in conformity with the pace of the aspirant's spiritual progress. It does not hold any point on the scale as having an absolute position in isolation, nor are all the practices suitable to the needs of everybody considering variations in personal temperaments and constitutions. Hindu rituals have embedded layers of meaning, from gross to refined, viewed according to the participant's station in spiritual life.

SANATANA DHARMA

In India, the religion is called *Sanatana Dharma* which literally means the *eternal religion*. There are two reasons why it is so called. (1) Unlike other religions, it has no propounder and consequently there is no specific date that it can be traced back to in antiquity. (2) With all the subdivisions of the religion, it can be said to incorporate the spirit of the diversities of world religions,[3] and can be equated to the eternal *Religion* itself. The Sanskrit word *dharma* means both man's nature and his religion. Thus, according to the Hindu, religion is a means toward establishing his real nature which is the fulfilment of the divinity in man, and is in an inner harmony with the world where he belongs. The principle of harmony itself is his God. The way to the realization of this harmony, of the one in many, varies according to the seeker's psychological make-up, determined to a large extent by the beliefs of the society he has been brought up in. As Sri Ramakrishna, a Hindu mystic of the nineteenth century, would say, 'As many are the views, so many are the ways.'

THE 'PERSONALIZED RELIGION'

Victor Frankl, a *guru* of modern-day psychiatry, refers to the 'profoundly personalized religion' that Hinduism is.[4] '... Hinduism recognizes that the temperament, needs, and capacities of the initiate himself in large part determine his approach to religious verities,' says Gordon Allport, the reputed psychologist, reiterating the point we have touched upon already. 'Although other religions provide personal counsel for the initiate at the threshold of maturity,' he continues, 'probably none goes to such lengths in making a close analysis of the youthful personality. ... Here we have a rare instance of an institutional religion recognizing the ultimate individuality of the religious sentiment.'[5]

KARMA

Like Judaism, Christianity and Islam, Hinduism believes that life does not end with death. The Hindus hold that everybody has a chance of being born again to undo the mistakes committed in past lives. The form of the future life is determined by the actions performed in previous births.

CASTE SYSTEM

The majority of Hindus follow the caste system, broadly a four-fold classification of people based originally on four types of human nature: Brahmin (spiritual–introvert, i.e., *sattvik*), Kshatriya (spiritual–extrovert, i.e., *sattvik/rajasik*), Vaishya (extrovert, guided by the constraint of inertia, i.e., *rajasik/tamasik*), and Shudra (guided by the principle of inertia, i.e., *tamasik*). Different duties in life have been assigned to each group depending on the nature of the people, which, to a large extent, is determined by the family environment. Teaching and priestly duties fall to the Brahmin, protection of the country and maintenance of justice to the Kshatriya, agriculture and commerce to the Vaishya, and the duty of assisting others to the Shudra. We have to keep in mind that the group division is in the frame of reference of *dharma*, meaning religion and righteousness, taking cognizance of variations in human beings, viewed in the setting of the universe which includes them. The worth of any work in the perspective of *dharma* is measured in terms of the spiritual progress it occasions in the agent. It is, however, possible for an individual to transcend the hierarchy of social duties and become a renunciate, i.e., a *sannyasi* or *sannyasini* in his or her personal spiritual quest, irrespective of birth or background, only if one is ready for such a step. In the Hindu tradition a true renunciate has always been a guiding force for the whole society. People from all walks of life still flock in reverence to the feet of these holy people for guidance, of which psychological counselling in the world of today is but a feeble approximation.

Untouchability has unfortunately been practised by the Hindus for a long time. The reason behind this institution must have been a concern for hygiene and cleanliness at a time when germicidals were non-existent. Arguments have been advanced to the effect that it is not a part of Hinduism, because it goes against the spirit of universal love encouraged in the scriptures. Mahatma Gandhi tried hard to eradicate the custom and gave the name 'Harijans', literally, *people of God*, to the so-called 'untouchables'. The custom is very much on the wane with the rise of public consciousness coupled with the adoption of proper legislative measures. It will take some more time for it to be completely eradicated.

In spite of indications to the contrary in the *Mahabharata*, the caste system has become hereditary for a long time, and offers the basis for the choice of one's partner for marriage.

THE FIVE MANIFESTATIONS OF THE ONE

Hinduism has developed over centuries of dialectical discussions, and has come to encompass spirituality of a wide spectrum oscillating from theism, with its belief in a personal God, to an atheism that does not share such a belief. Most Hindus worship the divine in the five personal manifestations (*panchopasana*): (1) the sun, (2) Shiva (the static principle), (3) Shakti (the dynamic principle), (4) Vishnu (Krishna and Rama are His two important incarnations) and (5) Ganesha (the dispeller of obstacles and bestower of fulfilment). All Hindu deities reduce to these five and their associates, who in their turn are but one and the same. It is possible for a Hindu to believe in (a) a personal God with manifestations in forms worthy of worship, (b) a personal God without such manifestations or (c) an impersonal principle. The idea, again, is to awaken divinity within oneself according to one's inclinations and capabilities, in the pursuit of spirituality. To rule fanatic parochialism out, Hinduism has the mandatory practice of paying obeisance to all the five forms before doing a special worship of any one of them, highlighting the fact that divinity is one, though approaches to it may vary.

ICONS

Although their use is not a must, icons are accepted in Hinduism. An icon is allowed to serve its purpose in man's search for the infinite in and through the finite. One with a rare capability of establishing a relation with divinity directly does not need any icons. However, the less advantaged majority, and those who have a fascination for encountering the Supreme in forms, worship it in images on the understanding that the infinite, which is without limits, can express itself in all kinds of ways.

The images of Gods and Goddesses have deep spiritual meanings. Even the concrete ones, on analysis, turn out to be abstract symbols for the one divine principle. The black colour of Krishna or Kali means that they are not physical beings, but are beyond the perception of ordinary mortals because of their transcendental nature. The flute of Krishna stands for the inner beauty, harmony and rhythm of the universe, and the enchanting call of the divine to be heard at the spiritual level. The Ganges on the head of Shiva means the constant flow of divine bliss. His trident (*trishul*) stands for the state of equilibrium that the primordial elements—*sattva*, *rajas* and *tamas*—are in. The crescent moon signifies the gradual awakening of divine consciousness. We will talk more about specific icons later on.

DIVINE INCARNATIONS

According to Hinduism, divinity incarnates itself, whenever the need arises, to save humanity in distress. God is not only omnipotent, but is also the lover and the subject of love, who always responds to the inner call of the devotee. He has planned creation through an ongoing process of evolution, a concept the Hindus have been aware of since ancient times.

LOVE OF ALL LIFE: NON-VIOLENCE

In an endeavour at meaningfully and harmoniously relating himself to the world outside, the Hindu does not make an exception for animals, for divinity, he believes, is present in all forms of life—human or otherwise. Non-violence is so much emphasized in their religion that many Hindus do not eat meat. Mahatma Gandhi, the father of modern India, strove toward establishing the Kingdom of God (*Ram-Rajya*) in his non-violent way of Hinduism, following the dictates of the *Gita*, the spiritual backbone of the religion. He was one of a succession of leaders who have contributed, since ancient times, to the ongoing process of the religion cleansing itself of accumulated impurities of doctrine and ritual.

CONTRIBUTIONS TO THE WORLD

Scholars believe that the law of *karma* (meaning that present suffering or happiness is due to past actions), with its concomitant theory of the transmigration of the soul, was passed on to Buddhism and Jainism from Hinduism in ancient times. The two greatest contributions that Hinduism has made to the modern world are *yoga* and *meditation*. These techniques toward attainment of mental peace have been adopted by people across different faiths without abandoning their specific creeds. The contribution that is expected of the religion today is in terms of mutual understanding among mankind based on the acceptance of differences. Ninian Smart, the well-known theologian, makes the following remarks regarding his expectations of this ancient religion in the course of his analysis of the future shape of world religions:

> Hinduism itself then appears as the unifying force in world religion because of its all-embracingness. It contains, essentially,

all faiths and all forms of religious experience within it. It has evolved over the centuries a mode of life where different aspects of religion can live together in harmony. And with the Indian emphasis on non-violence it holds out a real hope of giving an ethical basis to inter-religious peace.[6]

2

Hindu Sacraments and Rituals

The specific manner of performance of the Hindu sacraments varies according to local customs in different parts in India. None of the sacraments signifies a conversion into the Hindu fold or into a denomination within it. The following is a summary of the general features of the rituals involved.

NAME-GIVING (NAMA-KARANA)

On the tenth or the eleventh day after the birth of a child, the priest performs the name-giving ceremony, invoking the blessings of God. Many Hindus, however, defer the performance until the first taste of cereals (*annaprashana*), or initiation (*upanayana*).

FIRST TASTE OF CEREALS (ANNAPRASHANA)

When the child is six months old, the celebration of offering it cereals for the first time takes place. The food thus offered must have been offered to the deity before.

FIRST HAIR-CUT (CHURAKARANA, OR MUNDANA)

This is the custom of having the child's head shaven. Often, the formal celebration of the occasion takes place at the time of initiation (*upanayana*).

INITIATION (UPANAYANA)

Boys of priestly families have their initiation by the age of fifteen, with the investing of the sacred thread, which entitles them to perform their priestly duties. Later on, they may have a second initiation at a time of their choosing, depending on their spiritual capabilities and mental constitution. The second initiation is open to every Hindu at some point of life. *Upanayana* today is not always common among members of the two other castes, viz., Kshatriyas (warriors) and Vaishyas (merchants). The sacrament of graduation (*samavartana*) is performed these days on the day of *upanayana*. In olden times the life of a householder would begin with graduation after the days of celibacy at the teacher's house following *upanayana*.

MARRIAGE (*VIVAHA*)

According to the Hindu tradition, marriage is a step toward spiritual perfection, with a strong emphasis given to the social benefits accruing therefrom. Very often marriage is arranged by parents, whose duty is to see that children are established well for the second stage of regular family life, the stage of *householdership* (*grahasthya ashrama*) that follows the restraint and celibacy of student days (*brahmacharya ashrama*). Consultation of horoscopes for match-making is quite common. The auspicious day and time of marriage are determined on consultation of the almanac.

Tolerance and adjustment are very much emphasized in married life. Divorce is rarely accommodated as an alternative. Marriage is considered as much a bond between families as between individuals. Arriving at the bride's place, the groom formally agrees to start the marriage ceremony on a request from her father or guardian. All assembled express their blessings. Marriage is performed when the bride and the groom walk around the sacrificial fire seven steps together (*saptapadi-gamana*). Fire is looked upon as pure, because it cleans, and the light emanating from it is symbolic of wisdom that dispels the darkness of the mind. By holding the hands of the bride (*panigrahana*), the groom accepts his responsibilities as a husband. Tying a knot of the upper garments of the two is an important part of the ceremony. The veil of the bride adds to her charm and grace. The groom also wears a covering for the head. Kissing has no place in a Hindu marriage ceremony. Kissing of husband and wife is to take place in privacy, for their personal relationship is not expected to be exposed to public viewing.

The keynote of Hindu marriage is restraint, as reflected in the practice of the couple sleeping separately the first two nights, and fasting till the marriage ceremony is over. Abstinence is practised on other occasions, too, as on days of special worship, including the night immediately preceding the beginning of worship, and on days of bereavement.

The general sign of marriage for a Hindu woman in North India is a vermilion mark along the parted hair on the forehead, while in South India the custom is to wear an auspicious necklace with special beads (*mangala sutra*).

FUNERAL (*ANTYESHTI KRIYA*)

According to the Hindu scripture the *Gita*, with the death of the body the soul does not perish. The body must be cremated soon after death, before daybreak. No one is supposed to have any attachment to the dead body. Exhibitionism is not permitted. Embalming the body or beautifying it with cosmetics is forbidden. Use of perfumes and sandalwood paste for decorating the face is common. The body must be kept pure, away from items like leather and meat. It has to be washed clean before cremation. It is normal practice that people wash their hands before touching the body. The feet of the dead person must be accessible to those younger in age, and in the case of a spiritual leader, to all the devotees as well, in order to allow them to pay their final respect by touching the feet. The custom of opening only the top part of the casket in funeral homes in North America for public viewing of the dead body, denies the Hindu this important way of paying his last respects.

White being the colour of peace and purity, white flowers and white clothing for men attending the funeral is appropriate. Tradition requires the body to be in constant attendance while the names of Lord Rama, Lord Krishna and Lord Shiva are chanted. Just before death anything that binds the body, such as a belt or a ring, is removed from it. This is a symbolic gesture towards paving the way to a free journey of the soul to infinity. The *Gita* is supposed to be recited to fortify the mind of the dying person about to start the final journey. Placing a copy of the scripture near the head is advisable. The whole atmosphere around the person has to be peaceful. No cooked food is to be eaten by the nearest relatives till after the cremation. Taking a bath is appropriate after the funeral. The ashes are scattered onto a river, lake or sea, allowing the body to return to the elements it had originated from.

For the renunciates, burial is an alternative way of funeral, for it is believed that *yogis* can come back to life with the passage of time, even though apparent signs of death are peasant.

BEREAVEMENT (SHRAADDHA)

The sons, unmarried daughters, and nearest relatives of the deceased person eat cooked vegetarian food once a day, men grow their hair and beard and put on white clothes as a mark of bereavement for ten days. This period of mourning comes to a close with the performance of a worship called *shraaddha* on the eleventh day, where the concept of peace is emphasized. At the end of the bereavement period men shave their head and face. Small balls of cooked rice with clarified butter and black sesame seeds (*pinda*) are symbolically offered to the deceased person during the *shraaddha* ceremony. A community feast marks the end of bereavement. Sharing one's savings with others through presentation of gifts (*dana*) to the *pandits* and the poor is an important part of the sacrament.

OBLATIONS TO FOREFATHERS (TARPANA)

For the whole fortnight during the waning moon period that ends with the new moon preceding the Navaratri festival (see 'Festivals' section for clarification), men remember their forefathers and offer them water with black sesame seeds. On the concluding day the priest and Brahmins are treated with special food.

3

Some Relevant Information

DIETARY CODE

A large number of Hindus take vegetarian food without meat or eggs, but with milk. Non-vegetarian Hindus do not eat meat of female animals out of respect for motherhood. Beef and beef-products are absolutely forbidden. The cow that nourishes us with milk is to be treated virtually as our own mother; the bull cannot be killed, for it is the mount of Lord Shiva. Pork also is forbidden. Alcohol is very much discouraged. Rinsing the mouth after eating is normal. Food partly eaten or even offered to a person cannot be offered to the deity. Food or drink tasted or sampled, i.e., touched to one's mouth, must not be eaten by another.

DRESS CODE

Silken clothing is considered extremely pure. Being a non-conductor of heat, it preserves the spiritual vibration generated during meditation or worship. Cotton clothing should be preferably white in colour for men. It is mandatory to bathe and put on washed clothing before worship. Simple dress is considered proper for all occasions except marriage. Women prefer saris to other styles of garment.

AUSPICIOUS OBJECTS OF SPECIAL RELIGIOUS SIGNIFICANCE

Word: OM, the sign representing Hinduism. The sound symbolizes divinity in its primordial form.

Sound: Generated from blowing of the conch shell, reproducing OM.

Wood: Sandalwood. Sandalwood paste is an indispensable item for any Hindu ceremony.

Leaves: Tulasi (*Ocymum sanctum*) and *bilva* or *bel* (*Aegle marmelos*). The latter are brought dried from India for *bel* trees do not grow in North America.

Water: From River Ganga.

Metal: Copper and gold.

Flower: Lotus.

Decoration: Pitchers, preferably of copper, filled with water and decorated with leaves of mango, banyan or other trees.

Cereal: Popped rice, which is thrown into the air on special occasions.

Language: Sanskrit.

Scriptures: The *Vedas* (including the *Upanishads*), the *Gita*, the *Ramayana* and the *Mahabharata* constitute the basic scriptures. The *Gita*, though a part of the *Mahabharata*, is taken as an independent scripture. For the devotees of Krishna and the followers of Shakti, the divine mother, the *Bhagavatam* and *Sri Sri Chandi* (the *Devi Mahatmya* part of the *Markandeya Purana*) also are considered important scriptures.

OTHER CUSTOMS

One must be bare-footed at places of religious worship, or during any kind of religious celebration. It is customary that one sits at an elevation lower than that of the image of the deity. One must be clean and be careful to wash the hands before touching the image. As leather is generally considered impure, leather belts and wallets should not be taken to places of religious worship or celebrations.

HINDU CALENDAR

The standard Hindu year is divided into twelve months starting with Chaitra or Vaishakh in summer and ending with Phalgun or Chaitra in spring. Approximately two consecutive months correspond to a season, which are six in number. A month is 29 to 32 days long. Each month extends roughly from the middle of the Gregorian month to the middle of the following month of the same calendar. The following chart links the months of the Hindu calendar with those of the Gregorian calendar, as well as the seasons corresponding to them.

Vaishakh	April–May	Summer
Jyaishtha	May–June	
Asharh	June–July	Rainy season (monsoon)
Shravan	July–August	
Bhadra	August–September	Autumn
Ashwin	September–October	
Kartik	October–November	Late autumn
Agrahayan	November–December	
Paush	December–January	Winter
Magh	January–February	
Phalgun	February–March	Spring
Chaitra	March–April	

The day for a Hindu starts from sunrise, instead of midnight. The auspicious occasions of worship and celebration are determined on the basis of lunar calculation within the frame of the solar calendar.

4

Festivals

Since Hindu festivals occur on the basis of a lunar calculation guided by a solar constraint, they fall on slightly different days every year. The following are the salient religious festivals of Hinduism celebrated widely in India.

MAKARA SANKRANTI (JANUARY 14)

Celebration of spring on the occasion of the 'ascent' of the sun to the north (*Uttarayana*).

VASANTA PANCHAMI (JANUARY–FEBRUARY)

On the fifth day of the waxing moon in the month of Magh, there is a celebration of spring (*vasanta*) when Sarasvati, Shiva–Durga and Vishnu–Lakshmi are worshipped. People worshipping Sarasvati, the Goddess of Learning, observe the day as a holiday from school.

SHIVARATRI (JANUARY–FEBRUARY)

A twenty-four-hour festival, including fasting, preferably without drinking any liquid, in praise of Lord Shiva on the day preceding that of the new moon in the month of Magh. Worship is performed four times over the night to Shiva in the form of *lingam* (the symbolic form) with *bilva* (*bel*) leaves, flowers and milk or water poured on it.

HOLI (FEBRUARY–MARCH)

A festival to celebrate the triumph of good over evil on the day of the full moon in Phalgun. Huge bonfires are lit at night to commemorate the burning of demoness Holika, who perished while planning to burn alive Prahlad, an earnest devotee of Lord Vishnu. This is also a festival of colours celebrating the sport of Lord Krishna with His devotees as they sprinkled coloured water on one another. The act symbolizes His showering of the bounty of spirituality in all its richness. People re-enact the play even today with the sprinkling of coloured water among themselves. *Holi* is also an occasion for the celebration of the burning of Kama, the Hindu Cupid, with the fire that emanated from Lord Shiva's third eye.

RAMA NAVAMI (MARCH–APRIL)

A celebration of the birth of Lord Rama, an incarnation of Vishnu, on the ninth day of the waxing moon in the month of Chaitra. Rama, the eldest son of the king of Ayodhya, chose exile for fourteen years to keep the old promise of a boon His father had made to a stepmother, who insisted that Rama be sent away, and her own son be made the king. His wife and younger brother followed Him in the exile, during which His wife Sita was forcibly abducted by Ravana, the king of Lanka. Rama rescued her with the help of the king of a monkey tribe after a long fight. The story is the theme of the epic the *Ramayana*. It is emotionally very affecting for devotees even today, and inspires them toward the performance of life's duties. Rama and Sita are looked upon as ideal husband and wife for their unflinching devotion to each other. Recitation of the story is an important part of the celebration.

GURU PURNIMA (JUNE–JULY)

On the night of the full moon of Asharh, a special worship is performed to one's spiritual *guru*, who is the representative of God leading the seeker on the way toward Him. Worship of the great Vyasa, the author of the *Mahabharata*, in the line of the *gurus*, is a part of the celebration.

RAKSHA BANDHANA (JULY–AUGUST)

This is a Hindu *sister's day* which falls on the full moon of Shravan. On the occasion the sister ties a sacred thread around her brother's wrist wishing him protection against any evil. The brother offers her his respect and love.

JANMASHTAMI (AUGUST–SEPTEMBER)

The birth anniversary of Lord Krishna, another incarnation of Vishnu, on the eighth day of the waning moon in Bhadra. Krishna was born in the dead of a stormy night while His parents were interned by the cruel king of the land. He wanted to kill the new-born babe, for he had reasons to believe that the child would cause him harm. Around the time the child was born, all the guards went into a deep sleep, the fetters and the doorlocks fell off by a spell of magic, and the father rescued the baby, bearing Him to a safe place across the river. A serpent covered the child with its hood, as if with an umbrella. The story of Krishna, who stands for justice and love, is contained in the *Mahabharata*, as well as in the *Bhagavatam*. It is customary to recite the story of His birth and also His playful boyhood on the occasion. People feel the presence of Krishna—the divine boy—in their own children.

GANESHA CHATURTHI (AUGUST–SEPTEMBER)

On the fourth day of the waxing moon in the month of Bhadra, a special worship is performed in honour of Lord Ganesh or Ganapati. This is a huge festival in the central and southern parts of India.

NAVARATRI (SEPTEMBER–OCTOBER)

The longest Hindu festival that continues for nine consecutive nights following the day of the new moon in Ashwin, in praise of Lord Rama. Continuous chanting from the *Ramayana*, along with evening performances from the episodes of His life, is held for all nine days. The last four are associated also with the worship of Goddess Durga (*Durga Puja*), the female principle of energy of the universe, to celebrate the victory of good over evil. Rama is said to have worshipped the Goddess, seeking Her blessings in order to overpower the evil force of Ravana, the abductor of His beloved wife Sita.

DUSSERA / VIJAYA DASHAMI (SEPTEMBER–OCTOBER)

The day following the end of the Navaratri festival marks the death of the demon Ravana at the hands of Rama. This is also the day of the parting of Goddess Durga from Her devotees. It is said that

Rama had made a special worship of the Goddess in order to be able to win the battle against the mighty Ravana with Her grace. In the eastern part of India, people embrace each other forgetting their differences, after having made their farewell to the Mother at the end of Her yearly visit. They also treat one another with sweets.

DEEPAVALI OR DIWALI (OCTOBER–NOVEMBER)

Festival of lights, celebrated on the night of the new moon following *Dussera*. Diwali represents the prevalence of light in the midst of the darkness that life often encounters. Worship of Lakshmi, the Goddess of Wealth and Prosperity, is carried out in the evening. Kali, the cosmic energy, is also worshipped. It is new year's day in certain parts of India. Hindus believe that on this day Lord Rama came back to His kingdom with wife Sita and brother Lakshmana at the end of their long exile, and jubilant subjects celebrated the occasion by lighting the city of Ayodhya at night.

BHRATRI DVITIYA, OR BHAI DOOJ (OCTOBER–NOVEMBER)

This is a Hindu *brother's day*. On the second day after Diwali, sisters honour their brothers and offer them sweets. In return, brothers give gifts to their sisters.

5

Hindu Worship: The Sequential Pattern

THE INITIAL STEP

A service of worship may be performed by a priest or a householder who has had *upanayana*. The priest who visits a house to perform a worship at an auspicious time sits on a clean piece of cloth spread on the ground, facing east or north. An image of the deity to be worshipped may be placed in front of him. This, however, is not mandatory. The formal worship of the deity begins with a general worship of other deities, and a declaration that a worship is being performed for a specific person. The body of the worshipper has to be purified to make it fit to receive the deity during the worship. Thus, due respect is paid to the parts of the body by name in the process of their prospective union with the divine. Deep breathing (*pranayama*) also is done for the same purpose.

INTERNAL WORSHIP

This step is followed by a short meditation while uttering a *mantra* that gives a description of the deity, during which a flower is held in the palms joined together in a specific posture called *the posture of the tortoise*. After the meditation is over, the worshipper places the flower on his own head and worships the deity within himself. In this position he offers his heart as a seat for the deity. A divine nectar believed to be flowing from the lotus of the head is offered to God as water to wash the feet, to bathe and to drink.

INVOCATION

Next comes the invocation ceremony of the deity, during which He or She is requested to come, stay and accept the worship. The worshipper confers sight to the clay image at this time, and life is established in the image, so it acquires the status of a special manifestation of the deity during the worship. Once the infinite is deemed as having assumed a finite manifestation before the worshipper in the concrete form of the image, water is offered to the deity to wash the feet on arrival at the place of worship. This is followed by offerings that indicate a joyful welcome and hospitality, consisting of wet rice, flowers and sandalwood paste for greeting, along with perfumes, flowers, incense, lamp and food, water to wash the mouth with and to drink, and betel leaves to mark the end of the symbolic dinner. More items can be added at this point for offering depending on how elaborate one intends the entertainment to be. The Hindu deity very often takes a human character and is looked upon affectionately as a part of the family. The whole process is a sacramental divine awakening within oneself, considered a preparation for a complete surrender on the part of the worshipper to God, so his whole being becomes an instrument for the free play of the divine without any hindrance.

ARATI

An important part of the worship is the *arati*, or greeting of the deity with a lamp, a conch-shell filled with water, a cleanly washed piece of cloth, auspicious leaves or flowers, incense and lighted camphor. *Arati* is performed by rotating each of the items clockwise in the following order: four times at the feet of the deity, twice at the navel region, three times around the face, and seven times around the whole image. This is a form of meditation on the deity culminating with a gesture of complete surrender by prostrations in front of Him or Her.

END OF WORSHIP

It is customary to light a fire and offer some clarified butter and fruit to the deity to be consumed in the flames. A remuneration is paid to the priest performing the worship, according to one's ability. The ceremony ends with a prayer for forgiveness if any formality has been skipped or performed incorrectly, and a declaration that it is over. The image, made of clay, is then taken to a river, lake or pond for immersion where it dissolves. The respectful ending of the image serves to establish the fact that it is a symbol (*pratika*) worthy of reverence, but that God is not confined to it.

This is a description of an *occasional* worship. For *regular* worship of deities to be performed every morning and evening, the steps of invocation, establishing of life, giving of sight, the declaration of payment and immersion in water are omitted.

The kind of worship described above is called *tantric* worship, as opposed to the *pauranic*, which is much easier to perform, for purification of the body and other paraphernalia are absent there. *Tantric* worship is forbidden to be performed by one who has not been specially initiated by a guru, for without instruction a devotee might corrupt both the worship and himself. For the *occasional* worship, the devotee is supposed to fast the whole day till the worship is over, eat vegetarian food the day before and practise abstinence on the night of worship and the night preceding it. During the course of the ceremony and even after it is over, devotional songs appropriate for the occasion are sung to the accompaniment of drums, the blowing of conch-shells and the use of other instruments. The music is only silenced when the worshipper is absorbed in meditation. Many among the faithful offer flowers together to the deity three times in succession uttering *mantras* with the worshipper. Special care is taken to ensure that a flower or food, once it has been offered to the deity, does not fall to the ground or is not trodden under foot. The devotee's fast is broken by eating food that has been duly offered, known as *prasada*, literally, *the satisfaction* (of the deity).

INFORMAL WORSHIP

The Hindu worship or prayer does not accommodate sermons. The *mantras* or sayings in both cases are well-defined, and there is little room for any improvisation or deviation of any kind in uttering them. Chanting the name of a deity individually or in groups is encouraged for informal worship. Often, people may congregate in the evening at a friend's place or in the temple, and sing devotional songs together, preferably in the proximity of the image of a deity specially decorated and garlanded for the occasion. Fruits and sweets may be placed in front of the image, and shared by the participants at the end of the worship. The informality of the occasion does not demand the presence of a priest.

Repeated uttering of the *mantra* that one received from the guru has to be done in absolute privacy, preferably silently. It is only in privacy that one can offer one's individual prayers in words that come from the heart. Internal worship, which is the least formal, is always preferred to the external. Even the requirement of putting on washed clothing does not apply to it. Meditation in the sitting posture with eyes closed is a kind of internal worship.

6
Meaning of Icons

We have already touched upon the topic of the spiritual meaning of Hindu icons in the introductory section. In this section, we intend to deal with the meanings of the icons of four deities of Hinduism in some detail—Ganesha, Shiva, Durga and Krishna. We will not go into the historical question of how the icons came to take the present forms. Whatever value such a study would have in its own merit, it is irrelevant to the spiritual consciousness of the vast number of people who hold the icons in reverence.

GANESHA

It is customary to begin the special worship of any deity with the worship of Ganesha. The name means *the Lord of the people*. He has the huge head of an elephant, since He must contain all of spiritual wisdom. The elephant's dextrous trunk is used to handle both big things like a tree, or small things like a pebble, signifying that a *yogi* has to be versatile and make decisions according to the specific nature of the situation, without being mechanical. It stands for a discreet and supple intellect that adjusts readily to a situation with the ability to discriminate truth from falsity. The big stomach signifies the unconditional satisfaction of mind, which, though questioning, is full of bliss irrespective of what happens. The body of Ganesha, with its curved trunk, resembles the shape of *Om* in the *Devanagari* script.

Of the two tusks standing for the right and the wrong, one is broken. This means that the mystic mood transcends the duality of both. Thus, it is not in the acceptance of the one to the opposition of the other, but in their transcendence that spirituality lies. Problems of the moral dimension, that deal with right and wrong, are properly

GANESHA

addressed at the higher level of spirituality where the duality has been broken.

The deity has four hands of which the top left holds a rope which stands for our attachment to the pleasures of life that bind us, instead of allowing us the freedom which is our innate right (cf. Chapter 8). Lord Ganesha cuts it with the help of an axe He holds in His top right hand, once the individual is on the correct spiritual track and merits His blessings, indicated by the posture of the bottom right hand. The state of freedom is one of unconditional bliss which is signified by the sweet (*modaka*, literally, *that which pleases*) held in the fourth hand. He is both *the protector from obstacles* as well as the *bestower of fulfilment*.

Ganesha's vehicle is a mouse which is shown looking at the Lord in expectation, crouching in the midst of all the food that has been offered to Him. It represents the fickle mind in the thrall of its desires. Such a mind has to be surrendered to the total command of the deity. Then only can it serve the purpose for which it is intended, viz., leading the being to the state of spiritual freedom. Thus, mind, though apparently fickle, is the vehicle for man's spirituality, with proper discipline. The difference in size of Ganesha and the mouse poses the contrast between the finite mind and infinite spiritual wisdom.

SHAKTI (DURGA)

Shakti, literally *force*, stands for the primordial female principle of energy that is at the root of the changing world. It is female because femininity, to be equated with motherliness, is the sustaining teleological principle that heeds the basic needs of man which are spiritual. She is called *Durga*, for She is the destroyer of obstacles on one's spiritual journey. In the image of the deity, She is shown as ready to kill a demon that has originated from a buffalo which stands for the animal nature in us. It is only with divine help that man can conquer his animal propensities. The lion, the mount of the Goddess, represents man's virility. The animal nature is to be conquered and kept under rigid control, but never absolutely abolished, for everything has its part to play when placed in the right perspective. It is to be tamed to serve the purpose of creation as a proper vehicle of the divine.

MEANING OF ICONS / 47

DURGA

The ten hands of the omnipotent Goddess stand for Her protection of all the ten directions—north, south, east, west, north-east, south-east, north-west, south-west, above and below. She is always satisfied, which is the distinctive condition of a *yogi* with the highest of spiritual wisdom, and is shown smiling. She has a fair complexion which signifies *sattva* or morality at its best. At the top of the image the face of Shiva is indicated. With Her blessings, one reaches the domain of Shiva (*Shiva-loka*), which is of absolute peace. Thus, the dynamic principle (Shakti) leads on to the attainment of the static principle (Shiva) which constitutes the goal of human life.

Shakti assumes the form of Mother Kali standing on the prostrate body of Lord Shiva, and is extensively worshipped in that form in the eastern part of India. Here She is worshipped in direct conjunction with Shiva whose changeless state is depicted in His lying down posture. Shakti, the principle of change, is shown as standing on Shiva signifying that all the changes in the universe are rooted in the principle of changelessness.

Both Shakti and Shiva, the dynamic and the static principles, can be viewed from the macro and the micro points of view. At the macro level, She is the receptacle of the universe, its inner strength and energy, and the guiding force behind it. It is She who has planned human nature the way it is, with the potentiality of the individual self's final release through the attainment of Shivahood, i.e., the state of Shiva. At the micro level, She is the dormant divine force in its latent state of sleep, numbed as it is by the pre-spiritual state of the individual's attractions to pleasures, at the bottom of his spine. The task of the aspirant is to revive the force in the upward direction of Shiva who is on the other end of the spine, letting it pass through five spiritual centres on the way. Their union is marked by a divine ecstasy, a moment symbolized by the abstract icon of the *Shiva lingam*, where the snake coiling around the *lingam* (literally, *the mark*), symbolizes the upward movement of the latent force toward Shiva.

MEANING OF ICONS / 49

SHIVA

SHIVA-LINGA

SHIVA

The word 'Shiva' means *propitious*. The deity is depicted both as a static as well as a dynamic principle. In the Shiva–Shakti context, He is the principle of changelessness and a supreme state of peace and joy, attainment of which is the goal of human life, as we have already seen. In the dynamic aspect, He is the creator, preserver and destroyer of the universe. The *Nataraja* (King of dances) posture depicts the moment of His dynamicity. Here, the creator aspect is signified by the drum in the upper right hand, standing for the primordial sound. The preserver aspect is indicated by the posture of benevolence and *fear not*, of the lower right hand. Protection is granted consequent on the kindling of the fire of wisdom in the aspirant's heart, the fire that is held in His upper left hand. The fire is lighted with one's total surrender at the feet of the Lord as suggested by the lower left hand pointed to the feet. The dance itself and the fire encircling the image stand for the destruction of evil (*asura*) propensities once we open ourselves up to Him, for in destruction lie the seeds of regeneration toward the state of divinity. At the base of the image evil personified (*asura*) is shown as crouching under His feet. His trident (*trishul*) stands for the state of equilibrium that the primordial elements—*sattva, rajah* and *tamah*—are in, elements that point to the single spiritual principle at their base. The crescent moon on His forehead signifies the gradual awakening of divine consciousness in us. The snake means the awakening of the divine energy, as has already been indicated. The vehicle of Shiva is the bull which stands for our animal nature that has been brought under His total control.

The most abstract depiction of Shiva is in the form of a *linga* (mark) which stands for the principle of absolute changelessness around which all changes occur. He is the culmination of all our activities, right or wrong, which have a natural direction toward Him.

KRISHNA

The word 'Krishna' means *black*. As we have seen in the first section, the colour signifies that the Lord is not a physical being, but has a transcendental nature instead, above all manifestations of colours. According to Sri Ramakrishna, the famous Hindu mystic of the

KRISHNA, THE CHILD

KRISHNA

nineteenth century, He is black so long as we view Him from a distance. He has a permanent place in our hearts, bearing a more intimate and direct relation than any object of visual perception has with us.

The Lord keeps on sending His enchanting and beckoning notes to us on the flute even as we suffer, oblivious to His inner presence. The rhythm and beauty of life, however, are restored once we are aware of this sustaining presence. The awareness comes with the realization that we are ourselves the flute He has chosen as His instrument for divine aesthetic expression. While playing the instruments that we human beings are, He exhales His breath into us which is the breath of life. According to Lahiri Mahashaya, another great Hindu mystic of the nineteenth century, the Lord's playing on His flute signifies the *yogic* technique of breath control following which the aspirant attains divine realization, passing through six spiritual stages as indicated by the six holes in the flute.

The standing posture of the Lord itself depicts a superb rhythm showing the body bent at three places with the ecstasy of love. His crown has a peacock feather on the top, the circle in the middle of which stands for the third eye, also known as the spiritual eye. It is with this spiritual eye that He casts His glance of divine love on us. The whole mood is of a friend we must strive to relate to in all trust in expectation of His pure and loving company.

Another depiction of the deity is in the form of a little boy (the *Bala Gopala*) who is longing for our affection with His outstretched right hand. The asking is spontaneous, and the giving has to be spontaneous and unconditional too. Spiritual life consists either in the cultivation of friendship with, or affection for the deity, depending on the aspirant's dominant psychological disposition. The devotee is expected to sublimate his feelings and emotions in building a relation with the deity through the veneration of the icon.

7

Mantras and Prayers for Various Occasions

GRADUATION CEREMONY PERFORMED WITH PRIESTLY INITIATION

Teacher (*guru*) to disciple:

> Satyam vada. Dharmam chara. . . . Matridevo bhava. Pitridevo bhava. Acharyadevo bhava. . . . Shraddhaya deyam. Ashraddhaya adeyam. Shriya deyam. Hriya deyam. Bhiya deyam. Samvida deyam.

Speak the truth. Be righteous. . . . Look upon your mother as divine. Look upon your father as divine. Treat your teacher as divine. . . . Give respectfully, never with disrespect. Giving must be accompanied with a beautiful gesture, with humility, fear and sympathy. (*Taittiriya Upanishad* 1/11/1-3)

MARRIAGE

Groom to bride:

> Samrajni shvashure bhava
> samrajni shvashrvam bhava,
> nanandari samrajni bhava
> samrajni adhidevrishu.

Be a queen to the parents-in-law, sisters-in-law and brothers-in-law. (*Rig-veda*, 10/85/46)

> Mama vrate te hridayam dadhatu, mama chittam anuchittam testu.

Lend your mind to my affairs, let my mind follow yours. (*Mantra Brahmana*, 1/2/21)

A nah prajam janayatu prajapatirajarasaya samanaktvaryama adurmangalih patilokama visha sham no bhava dvipade pam chatushpade.

May we have a gift of children from Prajapati, may Aryama keep us united until old age. Enter your husband's place auspiciously. Be good to human beings, as well as to animals. (*Rig-veda*, 10/85/43)

Groom and bride together:

Samanjantu vishve devah samapo hridayani nau

May all the gods unite our hearts together. (*Rig-veda*, 10/85/47)

The relatives of the bride and the groom:

Ihaiva stam ma vi yaushtam vishvamayurvyashnutam kridantau putrairnaptribhir modamanau sve grihe

May you both remain here together without ever separating. May you live long lives and stay in your own home in all satisfaction with children and grand children. (*Rig-veda*, 10/85/42)

READING FROM THE *GITA* TO THE DYING PERSON

The Lord to Arjuna, His devotee:

Chaturvidha bhajante mam janah sukritinorjuna, arto jijnasurartharthi janani cha bharatarshava.

O Arjuna, four kinds of people have the privilege of worshipping me on account of virtuous deeds they have performed in the past (in this life, or before). They are: the one in distress, the aspirant, the seeker of wealth and the one established in wisdom. (Chapter 7, verse 16)

Yo yo yam yam tanum bhaktah shraddhayarchitumichchati, tashya tashyachalam shraddham tameva vidadhamyaham.

Whichever form a devotee wishes to worship with reverence, I bestow unflinching devotion on him or her in that form. (Chapter 7, verse 21)

Avyaktam vyaktimapannam manyante mamabuddhayah, param bhavamajananto mamavyayamanuttamam.

People with limited understanding consider me a person with form, ignoring my immutable, superior, transcendental nature that is unmanifested. (Chapter 7, verse 24)

> *Sadhibhutadhidaivam mam sadhiyajnam cha ye viduh,*
> *prayanakalepi cha mam te viduryuktachetasah.*

Whoever knows me in my proper relation with the universe and the offerings made to me, such a one's mind is fixed on me even at the time of death. Such a person feels my presence even at the final moment. (Chapter 7, verse 30)

> *Antakale cha mameva smaran-muktva kalevaram,*
> *yah prayati sa madbhavam yati nastyatra samsayah.*

The one who leaves at the very end, freeing himself from the body, keeping me alone in mind, attains me. Of this there can be no doubt. (Chapter 8, verse 5)

> *Yam yam vapi smaran-bhavam tyajantyante kalevaram,*
> *tam tamevaiti kaunteya sada tadbhava-bhavitah.*

At the final moment, O Arjuna, whatever form such a person concentrates on, when he leaves the body, attains God in that very form, for the person has been devoted to Him or Her always. (Chapter 8, verse 6)

> *Kavim puranam-anushasitaram*
> *anoraniyamsam-anusmared yah,*
> *sarvasya dhataram-achintyarupam-*
> *adityavarnam tamasah parastat -*
> *prayanakale manasachalena*
> *bhaktya yukto yogabalena chaiva,*
> *bhruvormadhye pranamaveshya samyak*
> *sa tam param purusham-upaiti divyam*

One who, at the time of death, fixes the life force between the eyebrows with unflinching concentration, devotion and an equilibrium of mind, meditates on the shining, supreme being, who is the receptacle of everything, the omniscient, the eternal, the ruler, and yet minutest of all the minutes, with a form that is not possible to conceive, self-evident like the sun, and beyond all ignorance, such a person attains that being. (Chapter 8, verses 9-10)

> *Omityekaksharam brahma vyaharan-mamausmaran,*
> *yah prayati tyajan-deham sa yati paramam gatim.*

One who leaves the body and passes away concentrating on me while uttering the mono-syllabic word OM, which is the same as God, attains the highest state. (Chapter 8, verse 13)

> *Abrahma-bhuvanallokah punaravartinorjuna,*
> *mamupetya tu kaunteya punarjanma na vidyate*

O son of Kunti (i.e., Arjuna)! Beings in all parts of the universe are subject to reincarnation. Attaining me, however, there is no birth again. (Chapter 8, verse 16)

BEREAVEMENT

> *Om Madhu vata ritayate. Madhu ksharanti sindhavah. Madhvirnah satvoshadhih. . . . Madhumanno vanaspatih. Madhumanastu suryah.*

OM. May the winds bring us happiness. May the rivers carry happiness to us. May the herbs and trees give us happiness. May the sun pour down happiness on us. (*Taittiriya Aranyaka*, 10/39)

OBLATION TO FOREFATHERS (TARPAN)

> *Om ye bandhava abandhava va*
> *yenya janmani bandhavah,*
> *te sarve triptimayantu*
> *maddattenambuna svadha.*
> *Om a-Brahma-stamba-paryantam yagat tripyatu.*

OM. Whosoever is my friend or foe, or was my friend in some previous life, let all of them be satisfied with my offering of water. OM. May the whole universe be satisfied.

PRAYERS

In the Hindu system, there is little room for innovations in group prayers, which consist in recitations of *mantras* or other sayings and singing of devotional songs. Here are some examples of a few prayers in Sanskrit recited in Hindu homes and temples everyday.

> *Sarve bhavantu sukhinah sarve santu niramayah,*
> *sarve bhadraani pashyantu*
> *Ma kashchit duhkhabhag bhavet.*
> *Om shantih, shantih, shantih.*

MANTRAS AND PRAYERS FOR VARIOUS OCCASIONS / 59

May everybody be happy. May all be free from ailments. May they see what is auspicious. May no one be subject to misery. May there be peace, peace and peace.

> *Om asato ma sadgamaya,*
> *tamaso ma jyotirgamaya,*
> *mrityor ma amritam gamaya.*

OM. Lead us from the unreal to the real, from darkness to light, from death to immortality. (*Brihadaranyaka Upanishad* 1/3/28)

> *Om bhurbhuvah svah tat-savitur-varenyam bhargo devasya dhimahi*
> *dhiyo yo nah prachodayat Om.*

OM. Let us meditate on the desired lustre of the creator of the universe who may kindly give directions to our intellect. OM. (*Rig-veda* 3/62/10)

> *Yo devognau yopsu yo vishvam bhuvanam-avivesha,*
> *ya oshadhishu yo vanaspatishu tasmai devaya namo namah.*

Salutations to the God who is in fire, water, herbs and trees, and who pervades the whole universe. (*Shvetashvatara Upanishad* 2/17)

> *Ya atmada balada yasya vishva*
> *upasate prashisham yasya devah,*
> *yasya chhayamritam yasya mrityuh*
> *kasmai devayaa havisha vidhema.*

Who else do we offer our sacrifice to, other than the God who is the giver of the inner essence and strength, whose command all powers obey, whose shadow is fullness, and death is verily His? (*Rig-veda* 10/121/2)

> *Tvameva mata cha pita tvameva*
> *tvameva bandhushcha sakha tvameva,*
> *tvameva vidya dravinam tvameva*
> *tvameva sarvam mama devadeva.*

You alone are my mother, O Lord of lords, you alone are my father, friend and close companion, you alone are my knowledge and wealth, you alone are my all in all. (*Prapanna Gita* 28)

> *Om janami dharmam na cha me pravrittih,*
> *janamyadharmam na cha me nivrittih*

tvaya Hrishikesha, hridi sthitena
yatha niyuktosmi tatha karomi.
I know what is right, but I have little inclination toward it. I know what is wrong, but I can hardly refrain myself from it. O my Lord, you reside in my heart, I will do whatever you want me to. (*Prapanna Gita* 57)

Mukam karoti vachalam
pangum langhayate girim,
yat-kripa tamaham vande
paramananda-Madhavam.
I bow down to Madhav (Krishna), the quintessence of bliss, whose grace makes the mute eloquent and the cripple cross mountains. (Ramanuja)

SOME OTHER SAYINGS

Ahara-nidra-bhaya-maithunam-cha
samanyam-etad pashubhir-naranam,
dharmo hi tesham adhiko visheshah
dharmena hinah pashubhih samanah.
Eating, sleeping, mating and feeling afraid are features common between man and animal. The former has religion as an extra distinguishing factor, bereft of which he is nothing but an animal. (*Hitopadesha*)

Matrivat para-dareshu
paradravyeshu loshtravat,
atmavat sarvabhuteshu
yah pashyati sa panditah.
He indeed is a wise man who looks upon others' wives as mothers, others' possessions as but lumps of clay, and all beings as oneself. (*Hitopadesha*)

Dharmo rakshati rakshitah.
Religion, when protected, protects. (*Mahabharata* 3/312/128)

Vasudhaiva kutumbakam.
The world is but one family.

II

HINDU SPIRITUALITY

God is formless, and God is possessed of form, too. He is also that which transcends both form and formlessness. He alone knows what all He is. For the sake of those that love the Lord, He manifests Himself in various ways and in various forms. Verily, He is not bound by any limitation as to the forms of manifestation, or their negation.

SRI RAMAKRISHNA

8
The Philosophy of Hindu Spirituality

According to the Hindu outlook, a human being does not reduce to a body and a mind. In the midst of physical and mental changes, there is a self which is beyond change. This changelessness is without a beginning or an end. Thus, birth or death pertains to the body, not to the self. This abiding principle in each person accounts for the human value system with its universal ethical norms.

We often have a tendency to look upon a person as if he were a machine in which the self is nothing but an item in the changing world. The consequence of this view is that the value of the person is reduced to such contingencies as the job or the sex of the person, his or her role as a husband, a daughter or a wife. Here the ethical standard tends to be individualistic, and morality is taken as synonymous with the individual's personal inclinations. The confusion in the human value system, rooted in the identification of the self with the changing body or the mind rather than as an immutable entity, is due to *ajnana* (literally the *unconscious*), which is innate.[7]

The expression *ajnana* naturally reminds one of the Jungian concept of the *collective unconscious*. The self, though mistaken for the not-self, has a tendency to be restored to the recognition of its true nature, a fact manifest in an abiding feeling of dissatisfaction that we have with our existing states of life. Material possession, whether for the purpose of actual or potential enjoyment, is not a remedy for our boredom and unhappiness, for it fuels the sense of inadequacy and lack of confidence that causes the unhappiness. The objects of pleasure ever fail to deliver their promise.

This is why consumerism, with its pre-occupation with material gain, breeds dissatisfaction instead of pacifying the mind. The unhappiness it generates is so thorough and overwhelming in its creation of a deep-rooted sense of inadequacy, that the situation can very well lead to a search for surrogate satisfaction from drugs. But the cry of the self has ultimately to be attended to at its own level, for its neglect leads only to further suffering. Here the behaviouristic model that looks upon the human organism basically as a machine and the deterministic model of Freud that looks for explanation of mental aberrations mainly in the infantile repressions, break down. According to the teleological Hindu model of the human mind, the self does not belong to the realm of determinism and predictability. The way its message arrives or is responded to, is not deterministic either. Here is a realm of freedom giving rise to peace, to be achieved through the realization of one's true nature. This is a realm of love and respect for all beings. The spirituality of man consists in the attainment of the real freedom (*moksha, mukti*), which also is innate or a priori (*sahaja*). It is a state of supreme bliss in which the self is freed from the limitation of ignorance. Human beings have to co-operate in heeding the calls from the deep unconscious level, and make deliberate efforts towards this state. It is a long journey, but even a little stride may save one from fears of the uncertainties of life.[8]

In opening up in the right direction, one finds a new meaning in one's involvement in the changing world, in one's job or role in the family. Ethical issues like abortion, the use of drugs and an unrestricted pursuit of pleasure are not decided on the basis of *likes* and *dislikes*, or accommodated as 'alternative life-styles'. 'Freedom of choice' yields to choice between the right and the wrong, with either of the alternatives offering its own consequences.

There are two kinds of forces working in man—the centripetal and the centrifugal, like the rotation of the earth around itself and its revolution around the sun. The turn toward rotation also indicates a turn toward revolution. The centripetal move in man tends to lead on to the centrifugal. In all the self-centred acts there are seeds of self-transcendence that lead on to the knowledge of oneself. This is the design of human nature. However, it is not all mechanical. Emphasizing the centripetal or the centrifugal aspects, or allowing a smooth flow of the one into the other is basically the individual's decision.[9]

The conflict between the right and the wrong, often personified as the *sura* (god) and the *asura* (demon), is depicted in the story of Goddess Durga's assassination of the *buffalo demon*. The outward fight of man oftentimes originates from his inner conflict, which is of the moral dimension. Thus, the battle of Kurukshetra, the stage-setting of the most popular Hindu scripture, the *Gita*, is taken figuratively as the inner battle that is constantly raging in one's own mind. The fight at the moral level can be won only if one takes recourse to the spiritual dimension. It is with divine help that man can emerge a winner. One must continue trying in order to receive that help. Giving way to frustration and despondency is exactly what Sri Krishna discourages in Arjuna in the *Gita*.

Meditation is a normal tendency in human beings, which is exploited by modern-day advertising techniques. Meditation on material things leads to frustration,[10] for it emphasizes the narrow *I* with its petty desires, leading to a constant clash with the *not-I*. The object of meditation has instead to be turned to the infinite *I* or God, where there exists no opposition, and no conflicts obtain.

Self-awareness comes with the knowledge of one's relation with God, who is both the in-dwelling principle, which is our source of peace, as well as the principle of change in the world. Mirabai, a sixteenth-seventeenth century mystic, describes Krishna in her songs as both the omnipotent Lord and the lover, who, according to the *Gita*, dwells in everybody's heart.[11] This is Hindu *existentialism*. The individual exists not as an *essence* of the narrow *I* where the self is identified with the non-self, but as a universal *I* in its mode of freedom. The path of finding the proper relation is existentially involving and long. This is why it cannot be imposed on anybody, just as appreciation of a song or a piece of art cannot. Spirituality does not consist primarily in what is done, i.e., the form of worship, but how it is done. The path one follows is determined by the way the relation is viewed by the aspirant. It could be that of an intimate friend, of a parent to the child, or of identity, as in the *Advaita Vedanta*. Other relations are possible to develop with God as a starting point to establishing a deep involvement with Him or Her. For the thoroughgoing atheist, the path is extremely difficult, if not lonely, for he cannot develop any relation of love with God, nor can he expect divine help on the long and arduous journey.

Broadly speaking, there are three main ways to the state of freedom—the way of devotion, the way of selfless action and the way of meditation on one's true nature, accompanied by the constant practice of discrimination between the true and the false. These are called *bhakti yoga, karma yoga* and *jnana yoga*. Although they are logically distinct, they must be combined together into a common goal, as indicated in the *Gita*. A specific blend in concrete details is prescribed by the *guru* taking into consideration the disciple's capabilities.

According to the Hindu ethics, there are five basic responsibilities for every human being. These are to nature, to the memory of ancestors, to the teacher, to humanity at large and to all creatures. The responsibilities are technically termed as 'debts'. The ideal of a Hindu is to resolve all debts before death. Thus, proper actions have to be performed to meet these responsibilities, benevolent actions good for all living creatures, including human beings, in the fitting memory of the ancestors who we owe our existence to, in conformity with the teachings, actions that co-operate with nature instead of attempting to conquer it. Such massive failings of our time as ecological pollution and poverty arising out of human exploitation may be seen as consequences of not meeting these responsibilities.

9

Chaplaincy in the Hindu Tradition

Hinduism, as we have already noted, is not a church-based religion. There is no custom of attending a church service on a specific day of the week, if at all. The only occasions on which Hindus normally get together on a spiritual basis are the festivals and the performance of sacraments or rituals to which people are invited. These, however, do not have to occur in a temple. Marriages, for example, take place at home. There is little in the religion corresponding to the concept of evangelism, for conversion, as we have noted already, is not traditionally present in the religion. Chaplaincy service is performed in an open kind of situation befitting the inherent style of Hindu ministration. It is in the setting of these words that we have to look at chaplaincy service in the Hindu tradition.

Spiritual counselling is provided only when it is being sought. This, again, is provided mainly by the *guru*, who gives the initiation. Counselling from a priest generally takes the form of readings from a scripture of the subject's liking, with explanations. The *Gita* is considered especially relevant here because it deals with the duties of life in conformity with one's spiritual ability. The whole process of counselling is future-oriented, so that the mistakes of the past are 'burnt' in the fire of spiritual wisdom to be generated with the help of the chaplain. This is achieved without going into the specific details of the individual's past. Here the direction is definitely not Freudian. Accepting the unavoidable suffering of life without anger and despondency is a goal of the Hindu life for God, the Benevolent, is providential, and Hindu counselling naturally emphasizes this fact.

To fortify the mind of the patient or the inmate, *mantras* are chanted in his or her presence, poems like the *Adyastotra* and *Hanumanchalisa* or hymns, are recited and sung, a special worship may be performed, and scriptures like the *Ramayana* or the *Bhagavatam* recited, filling the mind of the subject with holy thoughts. The chaplain lightly touches the head of the subject while uttering the *mantras*.

No attempt is ever made to 'convince' the subject of what is good or proper, for conviction must emerge from within the individual. Thus, chaplaincy in the Hindu tradition consists mainly in creating an atmosphere where auspicious ideas are likely to arise.

A chaplain who is responsible for the care of a person in spiritual crisis must, of course, be a patient and understanding listener. He may try to initiate a dialogue and be an active listener. In Canada or the United States, where the subject is far from his cultural roots, the dialogue with one of the same cultural or, possibly, linguistic background is presumably going to assume more importance in the act of spiritual healing. But initiating spiritual counsel need not compromise the traditional way of Hinduism. This consists in building an atmosphere conducive to the subject's well-being, in accordance with the practice followed through centuries. We have outlined the practice already.

10

The Human Value System—Ethics and Religion: The Hindu Perspective

THE UNIVERSALITY OF MORALITY

It is customary to make a distinction between ethics and religion in so far as religious dictates vary according to variance in religious traditions, but the core of moral dictates can be said to hold universally for every society. 'Do not steal' has to be an imperative for all societies, irrespective of their religious affiliations, though 'Do not eat beef' or 'Do not eat meat' relate broadly to Hinduism, Buddhism and Jainism, and not to other religions. A universal practice of stealing, as Kant suggests, does away with the institution of private property, that stealing is supposed to further. No such contradictions pertain to universal eating of beef, or idol-worship, which transgresses a very important commandment of the Judaeo-Christian-Islamic traditions. Similarly, one cannot be a Christian at all, not to speak of a pious Christian, without belief in Jesus as the Saviour, although such a belief is not held by people belonging to other faiths.

QUESTIONABLE RELIGIOUS PRACTICES

Such divergence of religious practices, which often oppose each other, have led to actions that might very well be questioned on ethical grounds. Conversion by coercion or other morally dubious means like bribing is a case in point. These questionable ways have often stemmed from the claim of exclusive superiority of religions over one another pertaining to objective truths which, however, are the domain of science. It is not surprising, therefore, that religions in their competition with one another for supremacy, received a blow with the advent and growth of modern science. Indeed, with the tremendous development in technology, science became the new religion guaranteeing power and prosperity. But science could not guarantee man peace which seems to be ever elusive and appears not to be attainable with technology at all. For, peace has to be attained through existential involvement with oneself in finding one's relation with God. Scientific knowledge, which is discursive in nature, has helped man 'conquer' nature to a large extent at the cost of earning his 'fall' from Heaven. Conversion is effective only when it is of the inner kind rather than of the outer. Consequently, there seems to be little meaning in comparing and claiming the supremacy of one god over another, and propagating the supremacy of one religion over the other. With the inner conversion, one comes to respect all human beings, irrespective of their race, creed or religious affiliation. Such a state is one of peace. The inner conversion brings not only 'tolerance' for other ways, but also respect for these other ways.

THE BEST RELIGION?

Let me dwell a little on the sense of pride in one's own religion. When I say: 'My mother is the best in the whole world', I do not compare with others' mothers, implying that they are inferior to mine. What I mean is that I feel so happy with my own mother, that I have little urge to compare her with others. This is not to say that there cannot be a best mother in reality, whose name may even have appeared in print. But this is all irrelevant in the context. I am not prone to any argumentation on this count regarding a counter-claim.

THE HINDU PERSPECTIVE

According to Hinduism, different religions are but alternate ways toward the same spiritual goal. Thus, although spirituality is a necessary quest for human beings, the religion one follows does not have to be the same for everyone. it depends on one's psychological make-up, the social dimension of which is shaped by the history of a race that one is born into. One's religion constitutes a part of that history. The nineteenth-century Hindu mystic Sri Ramakrishna Paramahamsa had a deep respect for Islam and Christianity, the religions he was exposed to outside his own. In the Ramakrishna Mission, founded by the disciples of the great teacher, Hindu, Muslim and Christian monks of the order live under the same roof. The practice, though unique in many ways, draws its sustenance from the tradition of Hinduism since ancient times. The first Hindu scripture, the *Rigveda*, dating back to at least 4,000 years, says, 'Truth is one, though the wise call it by different names.'[12] The *Mahabharata*, which includes the *Gita*, is replete with sayings meaning that religious streams, though separate, head toward the same ocean of divinity. In the sixteenth century, the universally acclaimed Hindu mystic Sri Chaitanya earned the deep respect of both Hindus and Muslims, but never initiated any conversion from one religion into the other. Lahiri Mahashay, another famous *yogi* of the nineteenth century, would initiate devotees from all religions into yogic practices, including the spiritual techniques of deep breathing, without demanding conversion to Hinduism.

By respecting religions I do not mean that all practices of religions, including one's own, are to be accepted as sacrosanct. If I see a religion founded in Ottawa today on the 'dictates of God' which requires its followers to carry a rifle or a hand-grenade to be used whenever the need arises, I would question the practice on ethical grounds.

THE CHAPLAIN'S SPIRITUAL SERVICE

The spiritual service that an inmate in a jail or a hospital or any other institution expects and deserves from a chaplain would not be religious, except, perhaps, for people belonging to the chaplain's own religious denomination. It has to be broadly spiritual. The question may arise as to how a chaplain relates to a murderer in a jail who does not believe in God, or to a dying person in the hospital who is an atheist. The answer is this. Spirituality is to be conceived in a very broad way, encompassing not only various theistic religions, but also atheism. For, if spiritual fulfilment is the end of life, it is there for everybody, including the atheist. According to Hinduism, the path of the atheist is very difficult to follow in matters of spirituality, though it is a valid one. God who can manifest Himself or Herself in several forms, or is a person with no form, can be viewed also as transcending the bounds of personhood. Here spirituality is atheistic, though there is a belief in the value of life which is embedded in its purpose. This purpose is not a materialistic one, for, with a belief in the materialistic purpose, one cannot existentially involve oneself in the expression of it in its process of unfolding. A mechanistic 'religion' that prescribes easy pills or mechanical devices, including free physical relations, for enlightenment and a journey to bliss, is not a religion worthy of the name. Here we find a parallel with the consumeristic society that guarantees the satisfaction of the soul with mechanical pleasure.

VARIABLE MORALITY?

Moral codes, in their turn, are not the same for all people, or for the same people at different times of history. The divergence, however, does not necessarily mean that a set of rules upheld by a society at one time is inferior to another contrary set followed elsewhere or at a different time. Kissing in public between men and women is considered ethically wrong by the people of the East, whereas the Western people of today even fail to understand the propriety of the custom. It is needless to say, though, that some kind of restraint in behaviour, including that relating to sexual interaction, is advocated by all societies. What specific form of restraint is adopted by a society at a given time depends on the history of its onward journey. Thus, ethical considerations, though universal, have not been addressed in the same uniform way at different places and times, which fact may not necessarily be attributed to moral frailties and lapses on the part of a people. If severe restraint is imposed at one point by a society, then there is slackening of the severity afterwards, which stage again gives rise to the demand for more restraint to follow. There may not be anything absolutely right or wrong in this continuous process of onward movement.

INTER-DEPENDENCE OF MORALITY
AND SPIRITUALITY

Truthfulness, forgiveness, respect for life, self-control, are considered virtues in every society, though uniform measures are not adopted to ensure them at a given point in time. The reason, as in the case of spiritual considerations, is that ethical involvement, like spiritual, is not mechanical either. The individual and also the whole society have to be existentially involved in such considerations. Here we can see how spirituality in a broad sense acts as a sustaining force and a guiding principle for morality. Thus, there is a mutual dependence. Spiritual activities, expressed in religious observances, have to pass the test of morality when questioned, as we have seen already. Morality, in its turn, has its life in the broader spiritual perspective. The main consideration against lying is not that universal lying is self-annihilating (that is, it will cease to be practised if everybody knew that others are lying, too), but that in lying the individual goes against himself. This, indeed, is a spiritual consideration. For those who believe in God, the goal of spirituality is finding one's true relation with God. For those who do not believe in God, the goal is finding our true relation with things and ourselves, a building of harmony within and without. Lying cannot lead us to these ends. All human endeavour, conscious or not, is toward reaching the spiritual goal of self-realization; ethical goals are only subservient to this broader end.

The dependence between morality and spirituality is clear when we see that those who are ethical in the right way, that is, follow the spirit of ethical principles and not just the letter, are better capable of reaching spiritual heights either in the theistic or the atheistic sense. Similarly, those who are spiritual have to be ethical at the same time. With spiritual advancement, ethical struggle diminishes, for spiritual progress leads to a meaningful relation with fellow human beings, and other animate or even inanimate objects. It confers a rhythm and harmony on life, and ethical dilemmas arising out of a tension between our higher and lower natures become minimized. Spirituality brings about peace resulting from a balance in life, including one at the moral level. 'Equilibrium is called *yoga*,' says the *Gita*.[13] Thus, although the same moral dictates are binding on all human beings, it is more expected of a spiritual person to follow the truth, and be an example to others.

VALUES AND THE CHAPLAIN

A professional chaplain is expected to hold a superior moral profile for a different reason too. A professional physicist may be a good physicist, though known to be a mean person and a liar. A doctor can be a good doctor excellent with diagnosis and administration of medicines, though rude and offensive in his behaviour. But it is rather contradictory if we describe one as a good chaplain who is a habitual liar. A necessary quality for making a good chaplain is honesty, and a habitual liar is not an honest person. The physicist in our example can be hired in spite of his moral lapses, because of his excellence in physics. But a chaplain cannot be hired for his excellence in chaplaincy in spite of his moral lapses. In fact, an interfaith chaplain, who administers broadly spiritual service to people of different faiths, is expected to be specially advanced on the spiritual plane, so that respect for human beings, irrespective of religious affiliations, is common nature to him. It is by no means a slogan, a technique in the trade, or a piece of information gathered at the intellectual level. Such a level of spiritual excellence will make him not only a priest of a denomination administering proper rites and rituals to followers of the faith, but will help him fill the spiritual needs of all kinds of people, soothing suffering souls in need of spiritual healing. Such a person will definitely have an exemplary character, not as a matter of challenge, but as a matter of course.

VALUES AND THE TEACHER

The role of a teacher, especially at the lower levels, has quite a similarity with that of the chaplain in a number of ways. He is hired not only for his knowledge and the ability to transmit it to the pupils, but also, equally importantly, for his capacity to enrich their lives in all respects, where the education of values plays a very important part. The pupils, particularly in the large metropolises in North America, come from diverse ethnic, cultural and religious backgrounds. The teacher is expected to have respect for the different traditions while teaching the universal values. Also, if the teacher does not hold the values in his character, he can hardly be expected to teach them. Thus, he has to be an example of the broad spiritual values in life to his pupils.

The teaching of values at the school level has to be within the broad frame of reference of spirituality. One must learn to be tolerant of other ways of life, keeping critical eyes open against a possible breach of ethical standards in all the ways including one's own. Children should learn to respect other religious traditions. Textbooks should highlight the salient features of religions that students find easy to appreciate. Universal prayers from diverse religious traditions could be shown as pointing to the same spiritual goal for humanity. The history of mankind, though full of innumerable, and oftentimes grievous, mistakes, could be suggested as a long and arduous journey to the realization of this very end. Krishna, the Buddha, Christ, Mohammed and many others may be indicated as torch-bearers on this journey in the long course of human history. The relation between ethics and spirituality in a broad sense needs to be pointed out. At the higher level of the school system, the question has to be addressed regarding the relation of the human value system and the nature of the human mind.

Classroom activities at the elementary level are primarily *action-oriented*, with emphasis on enjoyment through group interaction. While this process has its own merits, it ignores the basis of human nature, which is of inner and unconditional peace. Short meditations in the class, accompanied by deep breathing, done in a secular, non-denominational setting, would help develop this important aspect of human existence. With it will grow successful patterns of adjustment to crisis situations like divorce of parents, death in the family, sickness, and, later in life, retirement and eventual isolation with ageing. The teacher must have proper training in the methods of meditation and deep breathing. Meditation is an important tool for the discipline of the mind, and has been introduced at various levels in public life. It can very well be a part of value-education in our schools, providing a ground for self-respect which is a condition for respect for others.

RESPECT IN THE HINDU WAY

In the *Gita*, reference is made to the state of *prasada* of the human mind, which can be understood as the state of equanimity or acceptance that goes hand in hand with the critical faculty of the mind. Any change that is proposed or initiated has to rest on this initial acceptance. There must not be any kind of hatred, enmity, hostility or cruelty in the process. The political movement of Mahatma Gandhi was based on this concept, so that he deprecated all anger or hatred against the imperialist power. The culmination of the movement, he believed, would be spiritually beneficial to both sides. Respect for other ways of life must follow from such a state of acceptance, even when there is a need felt to bring about a change and steps are planned towards it.

The distinction between spirituality and its manifestation in religions has a parallel in the Chomskyan distinction of the deep level of the human language, and its expression in different actual languages. The deep level of language is innate, that is, given to us at birth independent of any experience. So are the rules of transition from it to the latter. Such a view of language gives us a glimpse of the human mind, the way it is constituted with its innate ideas. According to our analysis, however, basic human nature is constituted by its innate spirituality, the whole human value system being traceable to it, and the onward journey of all religions points to its realization in their several distinct ways. Some broadly common elements of diverse religious quests indicate the innateness of the quest itself.

III

HINDUS IN NORTH AMERICA

To study a banyan tree, you not only must know its main stem in its own soil, but also must trace the growth of its greatness in the further soil, for then you can know the true nature of its vitality. The civilization of India, like the banyan tree, has shed its beneficent shade away from its own birthplace. . . . India can live and grow abroad—not the political India, but the ideal India.

RABINDRANATH TAGORE

11

Hindus in North America

HINDUS FROM THE INDIAN SUB-CONTINENT

Language and Cultural Background
Hindus, like other South Asian religious groups in Canada, are a heterogeneous population in regard to their language and cultural background. They are first generation immigrants mainly from the Indian sub-continent, Fiji, the Caribbean countries of Guyana and Trinidad, and Africa. They began settling in the country in sizeable numbers only in the late sixties. In the case of immigrants from the Indian sub-continent, the language spoken at home is not English, at least among the parents, grandparents, uncles and aunts, although the children feel more at ease in English among themselves. Often the parents have a good command of English learnt as a second language, and probably used it as medium of instruction at the universities they graduated from in the sub-continent. The language most frequently spoken at home is Hindi or Punjabi, although there is a sizeable population who speak Bengali, Gujarati, Tamil or other languages. It is important to keep in mind that one can be a Hindu without knowledge of the Hindi language and one speaking Hindi is not automatically a Hindu. The languages are as different as English, Italian and Spanish, and they often do not follow the same alphabet.

The Hindu immigrants from the sub-continent generally came to Canada for economic betterment and occasionally for the furtherance of education. Although belonging to groups of different languages and cultures and with different socio-economic backgrounds, they share many experiences and concerns. By and large they are proud of the richness, antiquity and diversity of their culture, and are trying their best to pass it on to the next generation by promoting the teaching of classical songs, dances and music. There have been no political reasons compelling the Hindus to leave the Indian sub-continent for Canada, except for those from Sri Lanka.

Expectations of Children
Respect for the elders and the elderly and obedience to parents are very much expected of children. As is the custom on the Indian sub-continent, smoking and drinking in the presence of parents are not favoured. A number of Hindu parents continue the custom of abstention from alcohol and adherence to vegetarianism, and expect their children to do the same. Many who are traditionally non-vegetarian urge their children to continue the practice of excluding beef or pork from their diet, at least the former, if a choice must be made.

Continuance of the caste system is often favoured in the matter of marriage. Parents by and large expect their children to accept some version of the system of arranged marriage. Most of the first generation immigrants, after having lived in Canada for some time as unmarried men or women and established themselves, have gone back to the sub-continent to marry someone chosen by their parents. The custom of dating does not seem to fit favourably into this frame of reference, and Hindu parents generally find it quite unsettling. Parents are more concerned with their daughters in this area because of fear of unwanted pregnancy. Pre-marital sex, even with the use of protective medicines or devices, is not at all socially acceptable.[14]

Being disciplined and well-mannered is strongly emphasized among children. The use of profane language, especially in the presence of parents, is forbidden. All adults are looked upon as parents by extension. Children are used to living in extended families with grandparents and uncles and aunts. While this might lead to some conflicts arising out of a difference in value systems because of generation gaps, complicated by the fact of immigration to a new country, it enhances their abilities at social interaction with people of diverse age-groups. The atmosphere, however, at times tends to be over-protective. In an extended family situation, the child may not, for example, have mastered as simple a skill as tying his shoe-laces at an early age. Such a family is so close-knit a unit that any member of the family may show up for parents' interviews at school instead of parents. Parents prefer taking their children with them to parties instead of leaving them with baby-sitters at home. They do not mind if the party becomes a bit noisy as a result. They very often shy away from parties where children are not allowed.

Traditionally, education is deeply respected. Parents feel much pride in seeing their children do well at school. They are not always very clear, however, about the differences of pedagogic methods between Canada and the old country. Some are concerned about the 'lack of intellectual challenge' for their children in this system of education. Very often, however, mastering the *techniques* of abstract mathematical calculations, and memorizing information are looked upon as intellectually challenging. Specifically, they are at a loss when they see that the children do not bring the amount of homework home which they themselves were used to doing in India. They miss the opportunity of reviewing the lessons and events of the school-day with their children. This intense concern for the child does not necessarily indicate over-protectiveness, but is guided mainly by an emotion of love directed toward the child's well-being, and a desire to make the most of all possible areas of parental interaction with the child, including its academic field.

HINDUS FROM AFRICA, WEST INDIES AND FIJI

The situation is not exactly the same with Hindus from Africa, or Guyana and Fiji. Many from these countries had to come to North America for political reasons. Hindus have lived in Guyana and Trinidad for more than a century. Inter-caste, or even inter-religious marriage, though not necessarily favoured, is tolerated. Dating is accepted, though with caution and parental approval. Restrictions on drinking and on vegetarian diet are rarely severe, though drinking in front of parents is not encouraged. Eating beef is not favoured. Living in extended families is common and the attitude to elders is as described for the other group. Other considerations apply more or less the same way with the exception that English is spoken at home. Hindus from Africa and Fiji have features common between the two groups. Often they are bilingual, or even trilingual, speaking English, Gujarati or Hindi with equal ease.

ADJUSTMENTS IN CANADA

All the major festivals mentioned earlier are celebrated at Hindu temples and homes in Canada, though people often have to make adjustments with the time and mode of celebration in a country in which their religious practice is very much in the minority. For example, temples try to celebrate the festivals on a small scale on appropriate dates, but repeat the celebrations on the following Sundays to accommodate the large number of followers who might have missed the weekday functions. This would have been inconceivable in India, for special worships have to be performed according to the strict schedule of timing laid down in the almanac. The bonfire in conjunction with the *Holi* festival, the burning of effigies of Ravana on the occasion of *Dussera*, the large-scale participation during *Navaratri* for nine consecutive days and nights, and many important ingredients of other festivals are missing here.

Compromise and adjustment are conspicuous in the observance of sacraments and rituals as well. Sunday worships have become popular as a result of the need of the Hindus to get together on a weekly basis in order, among other things, to renew the feeling of cultural identity at a short interval of time and let the children share in this experience. Sunday is not a special day of reverence for them, nor is there a traditional custom of weekly congregation in Hinduism, for the religion is not church-based.

Many of the temples are trying to keep the doors open for individual devotees in the evening during weekdays. Individuals continue the practice of the community worship of Satyanarayan, a form of Lord Vishnu, or of Hanuman, the foremost devotee of Lord Rama, at home or at the temple.

HINDUS IN THE U.S.A.

The above account of Hindus in Canada may very well compare with a corresponding account of the people of the same faith in the United States with some differences. A major point of difference would concern the ability of the people to organize the teaching of heritage languages at schools in Canada in the broader setting of heritage cultures, where religion is an important ingredient. The courses are arranged on community initiative, and are funded and supervised by Boards of Education. They are a direct product of the philosophy of *Canadian Mosaic*, the achievement of which has been adopted as a guiding principle at various levels of governments.

Many of the immigrants, after having settled in a new country, Canada or America, are realizing that their cultural identity will continue for posterity, not through language, but through the broad understanding and practice of the religion. Hindu temples are being built all over North America, and congregations are being arranged at private places where such temples are not available. Although heritage languages are mostly used in temples, awareness is gradually rising that culture and language may need to be distinguished, and attempts are being made to explain religious concepts to children in English, which, for all practical purposes, is their first language. With time, awareness is growing of the organizational responsibilities of second-generation immigrants.

The estimate of Buchignani *et al.* is that between 80,000 to 90,000 Hindus were living in Canada in 1983.[15] The number must have approached the 2,00,000 mark in 1990, especially with the arrival refugees from Sri Lanka. Many Hindus in Canada are educated and have had professional training in India, West Germany, England or the United States. Some had jobs waiting for them in Canada before they arrived here. The situation is not very different in the United States. The number of Hindu immigrants there would be proportionally much higher. Many came as students, left their marks of distinction in their respective fields of research and scholarship, and were subsequently absorbed in professions where they have been acclaimed for their ongoing leadership. In Canada, however, one cannot apply for immigration from within the country. Thus, students coming from outside of the country, after completion of their studies, would not look for employment here. This consideration, combined with better facilities of studies in the United States, tends to attract a brighter class of students there. The net result is that the Canadian Hindu population as a whole has not fared as well intellectually when compared with their counterpart in the United States.

APPENDIX A

Hinduism and Other World Religions

Hinduism and Judaism are the two most ancient religions of the world today. Hinduism is monotheistic like Judaism, Christianity and Islam. The Hindu school of Advaita Vedanta is even monistic in so far as it identifies the creator, the creation and the individual subjects as one in their inner essence.

In Judaism, Christianity and Islam, God is transcendent. In Judaism and Islam, God never incarnates Himself. In Hinduism, God is both immanent and transcendent. He or She is manifest in forms and is without forms. In fact, God without forms is referred to in Hinduism as neither 'He', nor 'She', but as 'It'. God is believed to have divine incarnation, as in the Christian tradition, whereas in the Hindu faith there are more divine incarnations than one. According to the traditional interpretation of Hinduism, the latest incarnation is yet to come, like the messiah of Judaism, though He will come for the benefit of the whole of humanity irrespective of difference in faiths.

Hinduism and Judaism are not evangelical religions. Several times in history, Hinduism has given shelter to people of other faiths when they were inconvenienced with denial of religious freedom in their own country. In the *National Geographic* of May 1988 (p. 607) there is an allusion to copper plate inscriptions dating to the eighth century A.D. that offered protection to the Jewish people in Kerala by the local Hindu ruler. The community has ever since followed its faith without any hindrance from the Hindus.

Paralleling the traditions of Judaism and Islam, pork is generally forbidden in Hinduism. Beef is absolutely forbidden in the religion. Many Hindus are traditionally vegetarians, as are a good number of Buddhists. The soul is accepted as surviving the death of the body, as is the case for Judaism, Christianity and Islam. Hinduism shares the concept of rebirth with Buddhism so long as ignorance distances us from realization of our true nature, which is bliss. In Hinduism the importance of the *guru*, or the teacher, has been emphasized for help on one's journey to salvation.

In Hinduism, as in Christianity, the body is looked upon as the temple of God. In the former tradition, God is believed to be present in everybody's heart. By realizing this presence within, one can realize the divine presence without, and relate oneself in harmony all around.

According to Hinduism everybody's path is not the same, though realization of divinity is the common goal of all. One is expected to respect the other ways.

In the Hindu tradition the one absolute principle has two kinds of manifestation worthy of reverence: (1) incarnations and (2) symbolic representations. While incarnations are historic figures, representations are *archetypal* (to use Jungian terminology), helping aids, as it were, to hold the devotee's attention toward spiritual fulfilment. The fortunate few who are very advanced at the spiritual level may not, however, need the aids, nor do they have to depend on the theory of divine incarnation for further spiritual advancement. They may cease to have belief in the concept of the personal God found in many traditions, grounding their faith instead in an impersonal divine principle.

APPENDIX B

Centres of Hindu Spirituality in North America

Vedanta Society centres of North America are very dependable for information and instruction on Hinduism. The organization, founded by Swami Vivekananda, is about a century old. Names of all the centres are given below along with those of some other established organizations of recent origin.

CANADA

Maha Ganapathi Temple
1403-11th St. Edmonton
Alberta
[(403) 988-5161]

VHP Temple (Radha-Krishna)
3885 Albert Street
Burnaby, British Columbia
V5C 2C8

Bharat Sevashram Sangha
2107 Albion Rd.
Rexdale, Ontario
M9W 5K7
(416) 675-6049

Hindu Prarthana Samaj
62 Fern Ave.,
Toronto, Ontario, M6R 1K1

Hindu Sabha Temple
RR2, Hwy 10
Toronto, Ontario
(416) 793-2126

Hindu Temple Society of Canada (Ganesh Mandir)
10945 Bayview Ave.,
Richmond Hill, Ontario, M4A 2N9

Kali Temple
11762 McVean
Dr. Brampton, Ontario
L6T 3Z8
(416) 284-6734

Vedanta Society of Toronto
650 Meadows Boulevard
Mississauga, Ontario L4Z 3K4
(416) 566-5775

Voice of the Vedas (Vishnu Mandir)
8640 Yonge St., Thornhill, Ontario, L4J 1W8

Sri Lakshmi Narayan Temple
107 La Range Road
Saskatoon, Saskatchewan

CENTRES OF HINDU SPIRITUALITY / 87

U.S.A.

Vedanta Society of Berkeley
2455 Bowditch Street
Berkeley, California 94704
(415) 848-8862

Vedanta Society of Southern California
1946 Vedanta Place
Hollywood, California 90068
(213) 465-7114

Vedanta Society of Sacramento
1337, Mission Avenue
Carmichael, California 95608
(916) 489-5137

Vedanta Society of Northern California
2323 Vallejo Street
San Franscisco
California 94123
(415) 922-2323

Vedanta Society of Southern California
927 Ladera Lane
Santa Barbara California 93108
(805) 969-2903

Vivekanada Vedanta Society
5423 South Hyde Park Blvd.
Chicago, Illinois 60615
(312) 363-0027

Vivekananda Monastery and Retreat
6723 122nd Avenue
Ganges Michigan 49408
(616) 543-4545

The Vedanta Society of St. Louis
205 South Skinker Boulevard
St. Louis, Missouri 63105
314-721-5118

Ved Mandir
1 Ved Mandir Dr. (off Riva Avenue)
E. Brunswick, New Jersey, 08850
201/821-0404

Ramakrishna-Vivekananda Centre
17 East 94th Street
New York, New York 10128
212-534-9445

Vedanta Society of New York
34 West 71st Street
New York, New York 10023
212-877-9197

Vedanta Society of Portland
1157 S.E. 55th Avenue
Portland, Oregon 97215
503-235-3919

Sri Rajarajeshwari Peetham
RD 8, Box 8116
Stroundsburg, Pennsylvania, 18360
(717) 629-0481

Sri Venkateswara Temple
P.O. Box 115235
Pittsburgh, Pennsylvania, 18360

Vedanta Society of Providence
224 Angell Street
Providence, Rhode Island 02906
401-421-3960

Shree Meenakshi Temple
17130 McLean Rd.
Pearland
Texas 77584
(713) 489-0358

Vedanta Society of Western
　Washington
2716 Broadway East, Seattle
Washington 98102
(206) 323-1228

Notes

1. Cf. *Rig-veda*, 1/164/46, where it was said about 4,000 years ago: Truth is one, though the wise name it differently.
2. Cf. A.L. Basham, *The Wonder That Was India*, New York, Taplinger Publishing Co., 3rd edn., pp. 312, 347.
3. Cf. Ninian Smart, *Religious Experience of Mankind*, New York, Scribner, 3rd. edn., 1984, p. 580.
4. Viktor Frankl, *The Will to Meaning*, New York, The World Publishing Co., 1969, p. 154.
5. Gordon Allport, *The Individual and His Religion*, New York, The Macmillan Co., 1950, p. 12.
6. Ninian Smart, *The Religious Experience of Mankind*, New York, Scribner, 3rd. edn., 1984, p. 580.
7. If we reduce the person to the body that belongs to the world, we cannot explain the *yogic* perception of things past, future or far away, and one's existence at more places than one at the same time, as evidenced by the life of Lahiri Mahashaya. Cf., *Autobiography of a Yogi* (by Paramhansa Yogananda, Los Angeles, Self-Realization Fellowship, 1969), a good source of information on the great *yogi*.
8. *Bhagavad Gita*, 2/40.
9. Cf. ibid., 18/63.
10. Ibid., 2/62.
11. Ibid., 18/61.
12. *Rig-veda*, 1/164/46.
13. *Srimad Bhagavad Gita*, 2/48.
14. The South Asian institution of marriage is so different from the 'romantic' type of the West, that Westerners often find it very difficult to accept it, even at the intellectual level, as a viable form of marriage. If we analyse the form of the institution from the sociologist's point of view, we may discover the reasons why it accounts for so many happy, life-long unions among South Asians living in the industrialized West.
15. Norman Buchignani *et al.*, *Continuous Journey*, McClelland and Stewart, Toronto, 1985, p. 189.

16. Cf. Chintaharan Chakravarti, *Tantras*, Calcutta, Punthi Pustak, 1972, p. 55.

Glossary

ADVAITA VEDANTA. *Monism*, better still, *non-dualism*, of the absolute kind, according to which any kind of duality or multiplicity is false. This is one of the interpretations given to *Vedanta*, primarily by Shankara, the eighth century ascetic and philosopher.

AHIMSA. Non-violence to human beings, as well as to all living creatures, in deeds and thoughts. Mastery of its practice is accepted as an important step in the spiritual training according to the *yoga* school of spirituality. In the present century Mahatma Gandhi put it to a new use as a political principle in his fight against colonial power.

AJNANA. Ignorance. In the *Advaita Vedanta*, it is considered a positive entity with two functions: (1) *veiling* the truth, which is of the absolutely monistic kind, and (2) *projecting* falsity, in the form of diversities, where *one* is the only reality.

ANANDA. Divine joy, not to be equated with enjoyment of material things; the essence of divinity.

ARATI. A step in greeting the deity as part of the *external* worship, with lamp, conch-shell filled with water, a cleanly washed piece of cloth, auspicious leaves or flowers, incense and lighted camphor. It is considered the most popular part of the whole worship.

ASANAS. Commonly known as *yoga asanas*, they are the postures prescribed in the *yoga* system of spirituality, aimed at making the body and the mind fit for spiritual training through their practice. Some of the postures, like the *lotus posture*, allow the aspirant to sit in one position for a long stretch of time with the spine kept erect, thus helping the growth of the mystic mood. Western chiropractors and therapists are using or adapting many of these postures for the physical benefit of their patients.

ASHRAMA. A hermitage or monastery; a residential place of spiritual pursuit generally open to outsiders for participation in its programmes, where everything is held meaningful in the spiritual light.

ASHRAMAS. The ancient demarcation of four stages of life: (1) *Brahmacharya*, i.e., student days of discipline, humble austerity and celibacy during which a holistic education is received in a spiritual atmosphere for its application to life which includes the world with fellow inhabitants—human or otherwise. (2) *Grahasthya*, i.e., the life of a householder which encourages begetting children, and setting an example of discipline and compassion to them. A person in this second stage of life sees that his earning goes to the building and maintenance of a disciplined structure of society, including the support of renunciates who have given up everything in their spiritual quest. (3) *Vanaprasthya*, i.e., retirement from family life away from society. (4) *Sannyasa*, i.e. complete renunciation of worldly attachments.

ASURA. A demon, or devil.

ATMAN. The self, or the soul, which is immutable and not reducible to the body or the mind that are ever-changing. So long as the mind is not free from desires, it keeps on attaching itself to the self, after death of the body. A new body is formed as a result in order to allow the mind to fulfil its unsatisfied desires. Through the cycle of birth and death comes detachment, which signifies the end of the process, and the soul is finally released.

AVATARA. An incarnation of God in order to save the righteous in distress and destroy the evil forces. Rama and Krishna are the most important *avataras* of Vishnu.

AVIDYA. The same as *ajnana*. In *Advaita Vedanta* reference has been made to two kinds of *avidya*—the general (*mulavidya*), that accounts for the world to appear as real, and specific (*tulavidya*), that accounts for individual illusions.

BHAGAVAD GITA. Abbreviated the *Gita*, containing teachings of Lord Krishna to Arjuna on the eve of the righteous war at Kurukshetra, when the latter felt reluctant to fight his relatives. The Lord advised Arjuna to fulfil the duties of life with a total dedication to God. Some scholars believe the scripture to be a later interpolation in the *Mahabharata*, for such high-level philosophical discussions seem to be out of place with the course of the ensuing war. This consideration ignores the fact that Hindu spirituality does not exclude considerations of death or war, and that the ideas of the *Gita* are contained throughout the text of the epic.

BHAKTI. Devotion.

BHAKTI YOGA. The path of devotion as followed by the devotees of Vishnu (the *Vaishnavas*). The *Hare Krishna* people are followers of this path.

BRAHMAN. One belonging to the priestly caste, whose duties consist in studying, teaching and worshipping. In English, the name is often spelt 'Brahmin'.

BRAHMA. The first member of the Hindu 'trinity', the creator of the universe, a conception of the divine that is now almost obsolete.

BRAHMAN. The *Absolute*, which is considered as either personal or impersonal, according to interpretation.

CASTE. A division of the society, originally conceived according to the individual's nature, into four kinds: Brahmin, the priestly class, Kshatriya, the warrior class, Vaishya, the merchant class and Shudra, the class of assistants. Gradually, heredity and family environment came to play an important role in the determination of the individual's nature, and the caste system became completely hereditary. It did not remain confined to four either. Although vocational restrictions by and large do not apply any more in the caste system, marriage is still arranged on the basis of one's caste.

CREMATION. The general Hindu practice for funerals that requires the dead body to be consigned to fire. The body of a Hindu renunciate may, however, be buried.

DHARMA. Religion; also, the sacred law, according to which life is to be conducted to bring it in conformity with the *nature of things*, which, again, is another meaning of the word. *Dharma* also signifies *that which holds*, which means that following the sacred law, one becomes integrated in spirit and body.

FOUR ENDS OF LIFE. Gaining wealth (*artha*) and enjoyment of pleasure (*kama*) according to the dictates of the sacred law (*dharma*) leads the householder to the enjoyment of freedom and final release from suffering (*moksha*), which is the end of all human beings.

GITA. See *Bhagavad Gita*.

GUNAS. *Sattva, rajas* and *tamas*, the three constituents of *prakriti*, which in their combinations constitute the universe.

GURU. A teacher, especially, of spirituality. The *guru* holds a unique position in one's life. Having a spiritual *guru* is considered an imperative in one's life.

HARIJAN. The name given to the 'untouchables' by Gandhi, meaning *the people of God*.

HINDU. The word 'Hindu' is not Indian. It originated from an accidental mispronunciation by other peoples of the name of the river *Sindhu* which is situated in the north-west of the Indian subcontinent. The people around the river were eventually called *Hindus* themselves, and their religion came to be known as *Hinduism*. The Indian name for the religion now is *Sanatana Dharma*, meaning *the eternal religion*.

JATI. A caste.

JNANA. Knowledge, realization.

JNANA YOGA. The path of constant discrimination of right from wrong, and truth from falsity. It is generally misunderstood as a path for the intellectuals. Sri Ramakrishna followed this path, but he cannot be said to have been an intellectual.

KALI. A form of Mother Durga, depicted as standing on the chest of Shiva, the static principle, in whom all the activities of the universe are believed to be rooted. She has space as her garment (*digambari*), indicating the vast canvas of Her setting. This is why She is shown without any clothing on. She has a garland strung with human heads on Her chest each of which stands for the individual ego. It is only when one has severed the ego and consecrated it to Mother Kali, that one merits Her love and affection, indicated by the gesture of 'fear not' of the right hand. The severed hands in the form of a garland around Her waist stand for action emanating from the individual's sense of ego. Such action has to be deemed as belonging to the Mother who is the root cause of all activities (*mula prakriti*).

Only then is the aspirant's devotion complete. In the Western world Mother Kali is known as a 'violent goddess' who is associated with dacoits or highway robbers. The inner meaning of the image is rarely known or explained. Nor is the association of the great mystics like Ramaprasad, Kamalakanta or Sri Ramakrishna with the deity usually mentioned. The association only goes to show how the depth of meaning of the image has contributed to spiritual blossomings of the rarest kind.

KARMA. The effects of past actions, either in this life or before, on the present life of the agent or in a future incarnation.

KRISHNA. A principal incarnation of Lord Vishnu.

KSHATRIYA. The warrior class.

LAKSHMI. Vishnu's consort and the Goddess of Wealth, including that of the spiritual dimension. Her mount is the owl that cannot see things during daytime, but uses the eyes at night. The spiritual aspirant is incurious about things that ordinary human beings find fascination in.

LINGAM. Literally, a mark. In the religious tradition, it is the abstract symbol for Lord Shiva, the static principle, depicting the divine moment of the dynamic principle (*Shakti*) attaining the static. In the Western tradition, the symbol is interpreted with a sexual connotation. Very ancient historical questions apart, the Hindu mind is used to looking upon it for many centuries now as nothing other than Shiva Himself. Hindus practise extreme austerities in the form of total fasting for twenty-four hours without even water, and sexual abstinence for the whole day and the night preceding, on the occasion of *Shivaratri* when Lord Shiva is worshipped in the form of the *lingam*. It is customary for many of them not to have breakfast without offering water or milk to the *lingam* the first thing every morning.

MANTRA. A special saying in Sanskrit, often composed of apparently unmeaning cryptic symbols, for worship of a deity or for use as a mental accompaniment during meditation. The most common of all *mantras* is *OM*, which, though complete in itself, is also commonly prefixed to other *mantras*.

MATH. Monastery.

MAYA. Ignorance, the power of God, the principle that accounts for the individual's attachment to the pleasures of life in oblivion to the divine joy within. In the *Advaita Vedanta* it is taken as the other name of *ajnana* or *avidya*.

MEDITATION. Concentration of the mind, generally to the accompaniment of repeated chanting of a short *mantra* within; a state of serenity and peace.

MOKSHA. Release from suffering which is due to ignorance.

NIRVIKALPAKA SAMADHI. The state of bliss where the distinction between the knower, the known and the knowledge itself lapses.

OCHRE ROBE. The dress donned by a *sannyasi* (male renunciate) or a *sannyasini* (female renunciate). The colour signifies the flame that purifies.

OM. The most important of all Hindu *mantras*, standing for the primordial sound, comprising three letters—*A*, *U* and *M*, meaning creation, preservation and destruction respectively. The blowing of the conch-shell produces the sound, and is so considered an auspicious practice on all religious occasions. In its written form, *Om* may be considered as a logo for Hinduism. It is depicted on the front cover of the book.

PANDIT. A scholar.

PARA VIDYA. The subject of spirituality, considered higher than scientific knowledge (*apara vidya*).

PURANAS. The mythological narratives connected with the Hindu religious tradition.

PRAKRITI. The dynamic mechanical principle in the *Samkhya-Yoga* system of spirituality that accounts for creation and destruction through the process of evolution and involution.

PUJA. The Hindu worship, which takes the external form in the worship of an icon with flower, water and other items, and the internal form comprising meditation on the icon in one's own mind, imagining the body of the worshipper as the temple of the divine. External *puja* is of two kinds—*regular*, which is performed at least twice a day, in the morning and the evening, and *occasional*. It is customary to dispose of the icon used for the occasional worship after the worship is over. The icon for regular worship at home is looked upon as a member of the family who deserves special respect. Throughout the day, bathing, feeding, putting to sleep and waking up are supposed to be part of the ongoing care of the deity. One is expected to be full of the thought of the deity all times, so that every moment becomes a moment of meditation of the divine.

PURUSHA. The static principle in the *Samkhya-Yoga* system of spirituality that stands for the individual self.

RAJA YOGA. The path of postures, breath control and meditation.

RAJAS. An ingredient of the universe consisting of dynamicity, which is of the nature of suffering.

RAMA. One of the two main incarnations of Vishnu

RAMAYANA. The great epic poem, originally composed by the sage Valmiki in Sanskrit on the life of Lord Rama. Later on, the book was translated into the vernaculars of India. Of all the translations, the Hindi version by Sage Tulasidas has assumed a unique position for its emphasis on devotion not to be found in the original. In North India it is quite customary to recite the *Tulsi Ramayana* on any kind of religious occasion. The *Ramayana* has been translated into non-Indian languages since ancient times.

RIG-VEDA. The first of the four Vedas, comprising, among other things, hymns.

RISHIS. Sages, wise men to whom truth was revealed in ancient times, and later on contained in the *Vedas*.

SACRED THREAD. The thread received by the Brahmin at the time of initiation, hanging from the left shoulder and under the right arm.

SADHAKA. The spiritual aspirant.

SADHANA. Asceticism, spiritual discipline.

SADHU. A holy man, an ascetic, a monk.

SAMADHI. The state of union with God.

SAMSARA. The phenomenal world.

SANATANA DHARMA. Literally, *the eternal religion*, the name by which Hinduism is known among the Hindus.

SANNYASI. A holy man in an ochre robe who has renounced the world. The *sannyasi* performs his own funeral before he is initiated, signifying the death of his previous existence and rebirth into the state of divinity. The life of a *sannyasi* is preceded by that of *brahmacharya*, i.e., discipline, including abstinence—a screening period often extending to ten years or more. Although there have been excellent intellectuals among *sannyasis*, intellectual pursuit is not their main aim. Direct apprehension of God is what they are after. A *sannyasi* does not belong to any caste.

SANNYASINI. A holy woman who has renounced the world.

SARASVATI. The Goddess of Learning, a consort of Vishnu. Her mount is the swan that has the mythical power of separating milk from water mixed with it. An aspirant has to learn the technique of separating truth from falsity that are confused in life.

SAT-CHIT-ANANDA. Existence, Consciousness and Bliss—the essence of all beings, the other name of God.

SATTVA. The principle of goodness, one of the three constituents of the universe, predominance of which in life is sought after by the aspirant for the attainment of a balance in the midst of all disturbances.

SHAKTI. Power, the female principle of energy, personified in the form of Mother Durga or Kali.

SHANTI. The most widely used Sanskrit word after *OM*, meaning *peace*, often suffixed three times after a religious utterance.

SHRADDHA. The worship marking the end of bereavement. It consists of rites in commemoration of ancestors which are also performed on other occasions, as before marriage.

SHIVA. One of the five deities of Hinduism, the static principle of the universe.

SHIVA-LINGA. See *Linga*.

SHRI. Prefixed to the name of a man, exactly corresponding to *Mr* in English; the other name of Lakshmi.

SHRIMAD BHAGAVAD GITA. See *Bhagavad Gita*.

SHRUTI. The other name of the *Vedas*, which were revealed to the *rishis*, and are not of human authorship.

SHUDRA. The fourth class of people in the Hindu caste system who assist those of the other three classes.

SURA. A god.

SWAMI. A renunciate.

TAMAS. The principle of lethargy or darkness, the third constituent of the universe.

TANTRAS. Texts connected with the discipline known as *Tantricism*.

TANTRICISM. A type of Hindu spiritual practice that holds, against asceticism, that it is possible, and quite advisable, to attain the highest truth through restrained enjoyment and marriage. It has a sub-type which advocates the following of an extreme path for spiritual benefit. Such practice has traditionally been very suspect among Hindus, and the scriptures of the type itself restrict the use of the extreme path.[16] Hindus have made all experiments with spirituality and have cautioned of the excesses involved.

TRIMURTI. The *trinity* of Hinduism, now obsolete, consisting of Brahma, the creator, Vishnu, the preserver and Shiva, the destroyer. Brahma is virtually obsolete, except as a matter of historical legacy, and the other two are responsible for all three functions of creation, preservation and destruction themselves.

UPANISHADS. The last part of each of the *Vedas*, consisting of philosophical discussions, also known as the *Vedanta*. Different schools of Hinduism have offered different interpretations of the *Upanishads*.

VAISHNAVAS. The followers of Vishnu, or His incarnations.

VAISHYA. People belonging to the third class of the Hindu fold, who take charge of agriculture and commerce.

VARNAS. The four classes of Hindu society.

VEDANTA. The last part of each of the *Vedas*, also known as the *Upanishads*.

VISHNU. One of the five deities of Hinduism. His main incarnations are Rama and Krishna.

Bibliography

Bhagavadgita: The Song of God. Translated from the original Sanskrit by Swami Prabhavananda and Christopher Isherwood, with an introduction by Aldous Huxley. Sri Ramakrishna Math, Madras, 1969.

Norman Buchignani et al., *Continuous Journey: A Social History of South Asians in Canada*. McClelland and Stewart, Toronto, 1985.
This is an interesting book on the history of South Asians, including Hindus, in Canada.

The Gospel of Sri Ramakrishna. Translated from the original Bengali by Swami Nikhilananda. Ramakrishna-Vivekananda Centre, New York, 1977.
The book records the day-to-day teachings of Sri Ramakrishna, the extraordinary holy man of present-day Hinduism, believed to be an incarnation of God by his followers. It is an excellent source of acquaintance with the religion. There is an abridged edition of the big volume.

Swami Harshananda, *Hindu Gods and Goddesses*. Sri Ramakrishna Ashrama, Mysore, India, 1982.

Swami Vivekananda, *Hinduism*. Sri Ramakrishna Math, Madras, 1976.
The book comprises five lectures by Swami Vivekananda, the first, and still considered the best, exponent of Hinduism in the West.

Mahabharata. Retold by William Buck. University of California Press, Berkeley and Los Angeles, 1973.

Ninian Smart and Swami Purnananda, *Prophet of a New Hindu Age*. George Allen & Unwin, London, 1985.
This is an interesting treatise by a famous theologian of today on Swami Pranabanandaji Maharaj who established Bharat Sevashram Sangha in 1917 to consolidate the Hindus, giving them inspiration from their own tradition, and cleansing the religion of the accretions and abuses that had accumulated over

centuries. He is considered an incarnation of Lord Shiva by his followers.

Ramayana. Retold by William Buck. University of California Press, Berkeley and Los Angeles, 1976.

Rabindranath Tagore, *The Religion of Man*. George Allen & Unwin, London, 1931.

This is a collection of the Hibbert Lectures delivered by the Nobel Laureate poet of India in Oxford. Here the poet speaks in his superb style of the universality of the spiritual quest of humanity drawing profusely upon the resources of the Hindu scriptures, the *Upanishads*.

Swami Prabhavananda, *The Sermon on the Mount According to Vedanta*. New American Library, New York, 1972.

This is 'a fascinating and superbly enlightening Hindu reading of the central gospel of Christianity'.

Srimad Bhagavata—The Holy Book of God. Translated in four volumes by Swami Tapasyananda. Sri Ramakrishna Math, Madras, 1980.

Index

Advaita Vedanta 65
adyastotra 67
ajnana 63
Allport, Gordon 24
annaprashana 29
antyeshti kriya 31–32
arati 41

Bala Gopala 52, 54
bereavement 32, 58
Bhagavatam (the) 34, 38, 67
Bhagavadgita (see *Gita*)
bhai dooj (see *bhratri dvitiya*)
bhakti yoga 66
bhratri dvitiya 39
Brahma 15
brahmacharya ashrama 30
Brahmin 24, 32
Brihadaranyaka Upanishad 59
brother's day (see *bhratri dvitiya*)
Buddha 74
Buddhism 27, 69

caste system 24–25
Chandi, Sri Sri 34
chaplain(s) 16, 17, 71, 73, 74
chaplaincy
  in the Hindu tradition 67–68
Christ 74
Christianity 15, 18, 24, 69, 70, 84
churakarana 29
collective unconscious 63

Deepavali 39
Devi Mahatmya 34
dharma 25
dietary code 33
divine incarnation 27
Diwali (see Deepavali)
dress code 33
Durga 36, 38, 44, 46–47, 64
Dussera 38–39, 82

first hair-cut (see *churakarana*)
first taste of cereals (see
  annaprashana)
Frankl, Victor 24

funeral (see *antyeshti kriya*)

Gandhi, Mahatma 25, 27, 44–46, 75
Ganesha 17, 26, 38, 44–46
Ganesha Chaturthi 38
garhastya ashrama 30
Gita 27, 31, 34, 56–58, 64, 65–66, 67, 71, 75
God 18, 23, 24, 26, 27, 67, 73, 84–85
Guru Purnima 37
guru(s) 15, 16, 37, 85

Hanumanchalisa 67
Harijans 25
Hitopadesha 60
Hindu
  calendar 34, 35; ethics 66;
  festivals 36–39; sacraments and
  rituals 29–32; spirituality, the
  philosophy of 63–68; worship
  40–43
Hindus
  from Africa, West Indies and Fiji
  81; in Canada 82; from Indian
  sub-continent 79–81; in North
  America 79–83; in U.S.A. 82
Holi 36–37, 82

icons 26–27, 44-54
initiation (see *upanayana*)
invocation 40–41
Islam 24, 69, 70, 84

Jainism 27, 69
Janmashtami 38
jnana yoga 66
Judaeo-Christian traditions 18, 69
Judaism 24, 84

Kali 26, 39, 48
Kant, Immanuel 69
karma yoga 66
karma 15, 24, 27, 38
Krishna 17, 18, 25, 26, 31, 34, 38, 44, 51–54, 65, 74
Kshatriya 24, 25, 30

INDEX

Lahiri Mahashaya 54, 71
Lakshmana 39
Lakshmi 36, 39
lingam 36, 51

Mahabharata (the) 25, 34, 37, 38, 60, 71
Makara Sankranti 36
Mantra Brahmana 55
mantras 16, 40, 42, 43, 55–60, 68
Markandeya Purana 34
marriage (*see vivaha*)
meditation 16, 27, 40, 42–43, 65, 75
Mirabai 65
Mohammed 74
moksha 64
morality
    and spirituality, interdependence of 72–73; the universality of 69; variable 72
mundana (*see churakarana*)
mukti 64

nama-karana 29
name-giving (*see nama-karana*)
Nataraja 51
Navaratri (festival) 32, 38, 82
non-vegetarians 33
non-violence 27, 28

oblations to forefathers (*see tarpana*)
Om 33, 44

panchopasana 25
panigrahana 30
personalized religion 24
pinda 32
pranayama 40
Prapanna Gita 59–60
prasada 42
prayers 58–60

rajas 26, 51
Raksha Bandhana 37
Ram-Rajya 27
Rama Navami 37
Rama 18, 25, 31, 37, 38–39, 82
Ramakrishna Mission 70
Ramakrishna Paramahamsa 18, 24, 51, 61, 70
Ramayana (the) 34, 37, 38, 67
Ravana 37, 38–39

religion 17, 23, 28, 70
Rig-Veda 55, 56, 59, 71

samavartana 30
sandalwood 33, 41
Sanskrit 34
Sanatana Dharma 23–24
sannyasa 25
saptapadi-gamana 30
Saraswati 36
sattva 26, 51
Shakti 17, 25, 34, 46–51
Shiva 17, 25, 26, 31, 36, 37, 44, 48–51
Shivaratri 36
shraaddha 32
Shudra 24
Shvetashvatara Upanishad 59
sister's day (*see* Raksha Bandhana)
Sita 37, 38, 39
Smart, Ninian 27
spiritual service 71
Sri Ramakrishna (*see* Ramakrishna Paramahamsa)

Tagore, Rabindranath 77
Taittiriya Aranyaka 58
Taittiriya Upanishad 55
tamas 26, 51
tantric worship 42–43
tarpana 32, 58
trinity 15–16
tulasi 34

untouchability 25
upanayana 29, 30, 40
Upanishads 16, 34

Vaishya 24, 25, 30
values
    and chaplaincy 73; and the teacher 74–75
Vasanta Panchami 36
Vedanta 15, 16, 65
Vedas 16, 34
Vijaya Dashami 38–39
Vishnu 15, 25, 36, 37, 82
vivaha 30–31, 55, 67, 80
Vivekananda, Swami 21

yoga 16, 27, 28
yogis 32, 48